Dearest.

Xmas 1951

Another mus̶a̶ ... ly
Maybe you'll ... e.

Dad.

A

DOCTOR'S

PILGRIMAGE

Edmund A. Brasset, M.D.

A

DOCTOR'S

PILGRIMAGE

J. B. LIPPINCOTT COMPANY
PHILADELPHIA AND NEW YORK

Library of Congress catalog card number 51–11186

To

James E. Greenan of Wakefield, Rhode Island,
the wisest and most unselfish of friends

Acknowledgements are due to my editor, Tay Hohoff, whose skill and patience have been invaluable in the shaping of this book; to Beatrice and Jean Brasset, Louise and Hugh Cameron, Marion Joy and Al Macneil all of whom contributed encouragement and practical aid. And to George Boyle, a fine writer and my friend, from whom I have learned a great deal.

E. A. B.

A

DOCTOR'S

PILGRIMAGE

Chapter One

I DON'T know what I should have done if I had guessed
what the little man dressed in black, and with the black
briefcase in his hand, was bringing me that day when he
walked into my room in the interns' quarters at the hospital at Halifax. If I could have looked into the future, perhaps I would have gone out the window, made my way
down to the waterfront and taken the first boat I could
get for Easter Island or Madagascar, or better still, joined
the Byrd expedition to the Antarctic with a view to es-
tablishing a permanent one-man colony there.

But I did not do any of these things. I was merely curious and a good deal flattered because I recognized Dr.
John B. Thompson, a man who was something of a celeb-
rity in the eastern part of Canada. He was about five feet

four inches in height, of very slight frame—you'd think a strong wind would blow him away—and his lined face wore a perpetual expression of deep concern.

"I understand, Doctor," he began in a high-pitched, squeaky voice, "that you will be finishing your internship within a couple of months. Is that correct?"

"Yes, Sir."

"Have you made up your mind as to where you are going to take up practice?"

"No, Sir," I said. "I've been thinking about it of course —I was considering Halifax—but I haven't decided on anything definite as yet."

"Fine," he said. "I'm glad of that because I have a proposition that might interest you. Have you ever heard of a place called Canso?"

In a flash I knew what was coming and my interest sagged to zero. Certainly I had heard of Canso! It enjoyed the reputation of being the most desolate, dreary, poverty-stricken and shabby place in the whole country. "Fish and fog, fog and fish—that's all there is to the place," people said of it. I remembered hearing that Dr. Thompson had conceived some of his famous ideas for social reform after seeing Canso and that he had done a lot of work there, but I was not acquainted with the details. Now he was going to ask me to go there to practice and, I decided, I was going to refuse. I am no Grenfell, I told myself, resisting a slight tug from my conscience. I said cautiously that I had heard of Canso but I had never visited it.

"Of course not," he said. "Very few people in this country have ever seen the place. Why? Just because it is off the beaten track. It is isolated and difficult to reach. But it is a most fascinating place, Doctor, a most fascinating place! There are opportunities you would never dream of. Opportunities for doing good, for making a name for yourself, for everything! There are fifteen hundred people in the town and about two thousand more scattered around the countryside in a thirty-mile radius, and they need a doctor the very worst way. They need a young doctor, one who is not afraid of work, one who is not afraid of—" here he paused dramatically and fixed me with his eye, "anything."

Dr. John B. was a shrewd psychologist. I was afraid of plenty of things and therefore he had captured my interest. I took out a cigarette and lighted it, in an attempt to keep him from reading the expression on my face.

"Halifax," I said, "is a city I have always liked. Medical standards here are high. I think—"

He interrupted me.

"Halifax has more doctors than it needs. They tell me that there are dozens of young men in the city who are starving for want of work to do. It might take you years to build up a practice in a place like that and all the while people in Canso will be dying for want of attention."

He had something there. I was not sure that the people of Canso might die more rapidly for want of my ministrations, but I was, I must admit, afraid of the Halifax venture. I did not want to spend years building up a practice. For a definite and secret reason I wanted money and I wanted it within a certain time. Not just money in general, but a specific sum. I needed five thousand dollars in order to carry out a private plan, a secret quest, of my own. It was an ambition which had been growing in me— it seemed—all my life, although actually I had been fully conscious of it for only some six months. It was the Great Idea of my life and I did not want any undue delay in putting it into execution.

"Next to Halifax," I said, "I was thinking of Inverness."

"Inverness! Why, that's an awful place, Doctor. They

tell me the mine is closing down. Perhaps it may be closed already. A doctor going there wouldn't have a chance in the world. Now, you take Canso. The people there, it is true, may not have much money. But there are a lot of them for just one doctor. You would be very busy. They couldn't pay you much, but they could pay you a little and a little multiplied many times adds up to a lot. Look at those Woolworth stores! How do they make their money? A small profit on each item, but thousands of items."

I smiled at the comparison, but it impressed me just the same.

I said, "Inverness may seem like an awful place to you, Dr. Thompson, but I was born there and I kind of like it. Besides, the mines may not close. There have been rumors like that ever since I can remember."

"Well," he persisted, "will you come to Canso anyway and look it over? It won't hurt to do that much and you may be surprised when you see it."

"Well, perhaps, just to have a look."

"That's right. Just to have a look."

After he had gone I sat thinking for quite a while. When you are a medical student and nearing the end of your term, although you may have great ambitions for the future, you realize that at the moment you know very little. When you talk about starting to practice medicine on your own you feel like an impostor and you think that if people could see how little you know, you would be thrown into jail and kept safely under lock and key instead of being let loose on an innocent public. Therefore to have a man like John B. Thompson actually ask you to go to a place to practice, and tell you that some three or four thousand people need you and want you, is somewhat staggering. I was feeling quite important when MacMillan, my roommate, walked in.

"Mac," I said, "have you ever heard of a place called Canso?"

He looked vague. "It's in Labrador or Newfoundland or some place like that. Why?"

"It's in Nova Scotia," I said, "not more than two hundred miles from here, and it's a very important place." I told him about my visitor. I could see that he was impressed although he reminded me that John B. did not himself live in Canso and suggested that he might have some reason for disliking the inhabitants.

"Three months of your treatment," he said, "and half of the population will have disappeared underground. Hey! There's an idea. Perhaps he plans to use you to get rid of the surplus population for him and so raise the living standards of the people who are left."

After a while I went up to the fourth floor where I thought Miss MacNeil might be. Sally MacNeil was a student nurse in her final year of training and she was now on operating room duty. She was tall and slim and her eyes were hazel in color and very, very clear. She did not look like a movie actress. She looked better. An operating room nurse has it over a movie queen any day even though she may not be pestered for her autograph. Perhaps it's the ether that does it. Miss MacNeil was the only one who knew about the Great Idea, and now I wanted to tell her about John B. Thompson and Canso.

I had found that, somehow or other, after talking to Miss MacNeil I always felt a considerable rise in my self-esteem, as if I were really capable of coming to wise decisions and even, eventually, of attaining my ambition. This is a hard thing to explain, particularly as she knew as well as I did what a long, rocky road it was from a boyhood in Inverness, on the Island of Cape Breton, to the great height that was my goal.

If you take a map of the United States, in the extreme upper right-hand corner you will find the state of Maine. Above that is the Canadian province of New Brunswick and, to the right of New Brunswick, sticking out into the Atlantic like a long stone finger pointing at Europe, is the province of Nova Scotia. Travel east along the finger until you come to its very tip and you can look out across a few miles of water and see a remarkable island. This is the Island of Cape Breton.

Cape Breton is about half as big as the state of New York. It is all hills and valleys, lakes and streams, and is indented by deep inlets of the sea. Its shores are, for the most part, craggy and forbidding to mariners, who must approach them with caution hoping that the fogs which like to linger around the island will not sweep down and envelop them. The land is covered with spruce, fir and some maple.

Although the people who first settled the land were the French and some of their descendants are there to this day, most of the inhabitants are of Scottish origin. Their ancestors were the Highland people whom the English regarded as barbarians and savages and whom they fought for so long to subdue. They were, and their descendants are now, a race of people cast in a strong and rough mold. They live after a pattern very much like that of their forebears. Gaelic is a language that is still alive among them. The clans remain clans, although they adhere more loosely now than in the days when they fought each other and the English with claymore and battle-axe. They like to build their homes in the hills, out of sight of their neighbors and away from well-traveled roadways, as if they wished at all times to be prepared for a possible siege. They work only small farms although they have land in superabundance, and they live simply.

Travel up the northwest coast of the island—upper left on the map—and you will come, after some sixty miles or so of most thinly inhabited country, to a certain valley. It is a roughly square place. Low mountains enclose it on three sides and on the fourth side is the sea. In this valley lies the coal-mining town of Inverness.

At the present time Inverness has one mine working—in a haphazard and discouraged fashion at that—and there is the ruin of another mine, one which had ceased to operate before I was born. But in the years of World War I, when I was a small boy, things were different. I was seven when the war broke out, and just coming to be aware of things, and I knew—as did the twenty-five hundred other inhabitants of the town—that I was fortunate in having been born in one of the more important centers of the world. Of course, there were other more important places in the world, such as New York, Paris, London and San Francisco, but Inverness was no mean town. I remember that when we heard of the German advance on Paris, we thought, "If Paris goes, Inverness will be next!"

The mine, or "pit," was going full blast then and four hundred men were working there. There was even talk of another mine opening. Everybody said the place would soon be a city and that there would be trolley cars and everything. They were practically certain of it when a grist mill started up in addition to the mine and began to turn out flour. But the mill employed only four men so it was not much help after all, and anyway it only ran for about a year and then the structure was made into an office building.

I have heard that some visitors from the outside did not

think that Inverness was such a wonderful place. They criticized it because the main street had stores only on one side. On the other side were company houses, all exactly the same in shape and in color—a kind of gray. Also they said the mine or pit was too near the town, or that the town was too near the pit, and that the soot from the three tall chimneys ruined everything. They found fault with the main street and all the other streets because they were paved with cinders, and with the sidewalks, because they too were made of cinders. They did not realize that sidewalks like these are the very best kind. After cinders have been well tramped down by miners who are mostly huge Scotch Highlanders, they become smooth as asphalt and much cooler and softer for barefoot boys. But the visitors, unfortunately, never came in their bare feet and so they got a wrong impression. They said the stores were dingy just because they were covered with a little soot and you could not see through the windows. They even made fun of the railway yard and the two huge locomotives there, which they called pint-sized engines. Those locomotives were not pint-sized. Why, when one of them was on the turntable it took at least five or six of us boys and perhaps a few girls as well, besides the engine driver, to man the handles and turn it around so that it would be facing in the opposite direction!

The mine was directly opposite my father's store and only about five hundred yards away. It was a fascinating place. The huge boilers seen through the open door were frightening to look at when you thought of all that terrifically powerful steam trying so hard to get out and the steel plates straining to hold it in. It took a lot of courage even to stand at the door. Some fellows said they wouldn't mind going inside, but that was always when the foreman was in sight and they knew they would not be allowed to try it.

On the outside the compressor house was only a big gray wooden building, and if you were a stranger you might think it looked pretty shabby. But inside there was magic. It was full of enormous machinery. First of all there was the great flywheel, a hundred feet in diameter—some prejudiced people who did not understand machinery said it was only twenty-four feet—spinning for all it was worth. Then there were all the smaller wheels going around, rods sliding back and forth and long steel shafts going up and down working pistons and forcing air down deep into the workings of the pit.

And the Bank Head. That was something to see. When a full "trip"—a string of cars loaded with coal—came to the surface it had to move up an elevated structure beneath which lay the big railway coal cars ready to receive the coal. This elevated structure was the Bank Head, and several hundred feet back of it was the "hoist" with the big drum and its thousands of feet of inch-and-a-quarter steel cable that let the cars down into the pit and hauled them up again.

Certainly, if ever there was a town to stir the imagination of a growing boy it was Inverness. Not only was there the mine and the railway yards, but there were the mountains to look at and wonder what was on the other side, and the ocean to gaze at and wonder what was across. But even that was not all.

My father's store was not the biggest in town, but it was nearly the biggest. It had a sloping roof like a house, instead of a flat roof with a square false front as a store ought to have. I remember that this fact caused me no end of embarrassment. It gave me a distinct feeling of inferiority towards Fred Harrison, whose father owned a store that had the proper kind of roof and front.

But inside our store was wonderful. On the left as you went in there was the grocery section with its shelves of canned and packaged goods and the wooden counter with the cash register and the cheese cutter and the tobacco cutter and the ball of twine on it. Against the back wall were the barrel of sugar, the barrel of crackers, the case of tea and the barrel of chicory. On the right side there was the dry goods section. Here there was a glass showcase at least ten feet long and behind it shelves full of bolts of cloth. Suspended from strong hooks in the ceiling were clumps of pit-boots, teacans—bottle-shaped tins with cork stoppers which the miners used to take into the pit—and rubber boots. In fact there was practically everything anybody could possibly desire.

In the back shed, a place with an earth floor, were kept the puncheons of molasses and the tank of kerosene oil. When I worked in the store, as I often did on Saturdays and during summer holidays, it was here that I spent most of my time, filling cans with kerosene and drawing molasses. On a busy Saturday I was kept hopping from one to the other and I certainly had to keep my wits about me to keep from mixing the two. But somehow I managed it.

My father had been a seaman in his young days, on sailing ships plying between the West Indies, Boston and Halifax. He was tall, sombre and of commanding presence, and could more easily have been taken for a ship's master than for a small-town merchant. I know now that he changed his vocation because he thought that by doing so he could provide a greater degree of security for us, but I think that secretly he regretted it all his life.

My mother was a most remarkable person. Never had anyone such a capacity for making friends. She was of medium height, with pleasing features, black hair and sparkling dark eyes, and drew to her everyone who needed help or encouragement. She was so full of life, of sympathy and warm humor that it was impossible for anyone to remain downcast for long with her. In the evenings when the oil lamps were lighted and friends gathered around to pass a few hours, she would play the piano. She could do "Napoleon's Last Charge" or "Roses of Picardy" more readily than the works of Bach or Beethoven; and Paderewski I know could play much better, but I am sure that his Carnegie Hall audiences could not have loved his music one whit more than the neighbors who came to our house appreciated that of my mother. She was president of every kind of ladies auxiliary, of the local Red Cross and the various aid societies. At one time when the affairs of the town were in bad shape they wanted to make her mayor, but my father would not allow it. We were very much disappointed. We were sure that if mother were mayor, our town would be a city in no time and we would have trolley cars.

She had three standard remedies for healing the sick— goose grease to be applied externally for any kind of chest trouble; hot ginger to be taken internally for any kind of abdominal trouble; and geranium leaves for any kind of small wound, bruise or superficial infection. I was always getting into fights with other kids and there was scarcely a day when I didn't come home with some kind of bump or bruise. My mother kept geranium plants in practically every window in the house. She would snip off a leaf or two and, using the handle of a pair of scissors as a little hammer, tap it all over very carefully and gently to make the juice appear. Then she would apply the leaf to the sore spot and bandage it on.

How good were these remedies? Well, after so many

years in medical school and so much time spent in post-graduate studies and so many years of medical practice, I am not quite so sure about the goose grease and the hot ginger. I think penicillin is probably better. But for the bumps and bruises which a small boy takes home every day, I still think geranium leaves can't be beat. On one condition, however. They must be applied by your own mother.

I don't know when it was that I developed the notion of studying medicine. I believe it came on very gradually. I remember that someone gave me a book on the life of Louis Pasteur, and it was an entrancing experience. I suppose the lure of discovery has a fundamental appeal to everyone. I know in my case it was very strong. I had wanted to be an astronomer, a discoverer of new planets, and there was an interval during which I had been especially fond of reading stories of Arctic exploration. Now it struck me that the search for new germs could be just as exciting as the search for new comets and there was just as much glory in exploring the mysteries of the human body as in penetrating into the icebound vastnesses of the Polar regions.

Anyhow, in one way or another, the conviction grew upon me that medicine was to be my career. Over a period of time this became a consuming ambition. I forgot everything else in favor of this new interest, and worked at my studies with a specific aim in mind. At college I enrolled for the pre-medical course—two years of dissecting frogs, cats and dogfish, of acquiring knowledge of fairly advanced chemistry and physics, and of poring over more books than I can count. It was a grueling time, but in the end the preparatory work was done, I was ready for medical school.

It was 1929—a fateful year for many people—and one fine day in September I found myself in the city of Halifax, signing my name in the office of the registrar of the Dalhousie School of Medicine.

It took a little while to become adjusted to medical school. We were a class of about fifty, representing almost every part of Canada and a few of the New England states. We spent the first few days sizing up each other—trying to estimate the competition—because it is a foregone conclusion in all medical schools that out of every class, twenty to thirty-five percent are eliminated before completion of the course.

During the first few weeks we had to steel ourselves against the many minor shocks incident to our first introduction to the study of the human body. We adopted an irreverent vocabulary and irreverent manners in order to cover up our feelings. We spoke of the cadavers as "stiffs" when we knew they really were the remains of poor people who had been unfortunate enough to die without friends or money to bury them, and whose bodies had therefore become our legal possessions to work on and study. We made detestable little jokes. My dissecting partner who worked on the left side while I worked on the right, one day threw his "part"—the leg—across the narrow slab into my lap and I threw it back; only he moved out of the way and it fell on the floor with a heavy thud, drawing for me a severe reprimand from our professor.

One episode during this pretending-to-be hard-boiled stage I remember particularly. I was going downstairs from the anatomy lab when I encountered an attendant who worked about the place, coming up. We met on a landing. He carried a heavy pail, fairly new, made of galvanized iron with a partly detached label on it which said "Cap. 2 gal." Glancing at it casually I saw that it was full of human hearts. Immersed in a formaldehyde solution, they were on the way from the pathology department to someone upstairs who was doing a "study." It is true that the former owners of those hearts did not need them now and that they were going to be put to the best of possible uses—the advancement of learning—but how terrifically important they had been at one time. Each one had been more precious than all the diamonds in the world to somebody, and more important than all the stars in the sky. About each one there had centered the greatest of dramas—the drama of life. I don't know precisely how many there were. I have never got around to calculating how many human hearts you can put in a two-gallon galvanized pail.

The first few years of our medical studies were devoted chiefly to the basic sciences of anatomy, histology, bacteriology, pathology, morbid anatomy and biochemistry. Formidable they were—more so than I had expected. I had thought that anatomy, for instance, would be fairly easy—that you could take a bone, look at it and say, "This is a shinbone," and everybody would be satisfied. But no! It was a shock to discover that the tibia or shinbone rated several thousands of words in the textbook—all of which had to be committed to memory—plus lectures and demonstrations. "At this rate," I thought, "we will never get anywhere." And then it turned out that the tibia was one of the more simple structures and that every one of the bones—even unimportant ones which you'd think could have been ignored—got a similar treatment.

Take the eye socket in a skull. It seemed to me that any professor of anatomy should be perfectly happy if a student could put his finger in it and say simply, "This is an eye socket." But would he? No. You had to say, "The orbit is formed by the orbital plate of the frontal bone and the lesser wing of the sphenoid, superiorly; by the orbital surface of the maxilla, a process of the malar and a process of the palate bone, inferiorly; by the nasal process of the maxilla, the lacrimal, the ethmoid and the sphenoid, medially, and by the orbital process of the malar and the greater wing of the sphenoid laterally."

I had looked forward very much to dissecting the brain. Somehow I fancied that the answers to many puzzling things would be found when I could take apart the mechanism inside the human head. A day came when a small saw was put in my hands and I was told I might now open the cranium of my cadaver. I set to work with great eagerness and care and in the course of an hour or so was lifting off the bony cover and looking at what is admittedly the greatest earthly creation which we can see and touch. More than anything it resembled a gigantic shelled walnut, with the ridges, of course, more closely packed together and the grooves between reduced to mere slits. I had my Manual of Dissection, besides the bulky Gray's *Anatomy*, spread out beside me and I tried to identify landmarks on the brain before me by looking at the diagrams in the books.

One thing struck me immediately. There would be more questions than answers in the study of the brain. The diagram looked like a map of the Sahara. There were oases here and there which marked spots on the surface of which the function was known. For example, at the highest point, corresponding to the very top of the head, there was a small area—not more than a quarter inch in diameter—which was known to control movements of the legs, below that an area for the control of the trunk of the body, lower still an area for the arms and lowest of all, not far above the ear, was the center which controls the muscles of the larynx. For ease in remembering, I noted that a chorus girl at work must use the very highest part of her brain, whereas a singer uses a much lower part.

But these areas of the brain of which men knew the use, constituted only a fraction of the total surface. The remainder was all undiscovered country and the moment when I realized this was the most exciting of my life. Talk about the lure of Arctic exploration! This put a search for the North Pole in almost the same class as an excursion into one's own back yard. I knew now that I would be a haunted man for the rest of my life. Those vacant spaces in the diagram of the brain would give me no peace until I could fill in at least some of them.

Day by day, night by night, month in and month out, for three years we worked our way through books and lectures and cadavers and one day found that we had emerged out of the wilderness into the clinical years—the years when we actually saw patients, and learned to treat them.

With the beginning of this new phase, we began to feel a little bit like doctors.

Our teachers were now all men who were in active practice in the city instead of the full-time professors who had taught us the basic sciences. Up to now we had been in an endurance test. Now it was more or less taken for granted that as we had survived the grueling first years we would go through and finish. Accordingly our teachers began to treat us not merely as students, but, to a slight degree, as colleagues. Besides our formal instruction we were "let in" on some of the less formal aspects of the profession.

We soon learned that the profession is not one closely knit body. It is full of rivalries and there is an impressive system that can almost be called a "caste system." At least that is one way of thinking of it. The existence of this caste system was never told us in so many words. Perhaps many of our instructors never thought of it in that way, and many of them would be the first to deny it. Nevertheless it exists and we came to learn of it, first as a vague impression and then as an out-and-out reality.

The lowest "caste" in the profession is that of the general practitioner who practices in the country or in a remote small town. To the intern who reads his case reports on patients sent in to the city hospital for treatment—reports not always phrased in the up-to-date scientific terminology of the day—he is the GP or the LMD (local medical doctor). Although he is praised in the literature of the layman and receives open tributes from his specialist colleagues in the city at medical conventions where he is called "the man in the field," he is in general looked down upon, in a good-natured way, by the specialist. We used to hear lectures on the need for good general practitioners, on the important place they held in the general scheme of things and about how indispensable they were. Nevertheless we also heard many little off-the-record jokes about them. One of our instructors used to love to tell stories like this during a moment of relaxation in the middle of a stiff lecture.

"I used to know an old doctor down in the country, a fine old fellow"—they were always fine old fellows in the stories—"who was noted for being rather—let us say—economical. He told me one day that he always had every patient bring in a sample of urine every time he came to his office.

" 'Don't tell me,' I said to him, 'that you do a urinalysis on the same patient every time he comes in.'

" 'Of course not,' he answered. 'I pour it down the sink.'

" 'But why?' I asked him.

" 'Well,' he said, taking a pull at his pipe, 'I dispense my own drugs you know. The medicines have to be put in bottles and bottles cost three to five cents each, so—!' "

We all laughed. It was a good story and well told, but the teller had unintentionally dropped the G.P. in our estimation by several degrees. The statement that the doctor was a "fine old fellow" and the further statement that he was a peculiar character and not at all representative of his class, did not counterbalance the effect. Stories about the odd treatments used by the "fine old fellows" out in the field, were also good subjects for humorous stories. As time went on we gradually came to feel that to go in general practice was definitely an admission of mediocrity. So more and more, every student in the class began to think in terms of specializing. There was little talk now of "Where are you going to practice when you get out," but much talk of "What are you going to go in for?" We came to feel that our medical course was simply a basic foundation for the specialized studies that were to follow.

In the estimation of most of my classmates, the highest state that could be attained, and therefore the thing to work for, was the specialty of general surgery. This feeling was not decreased by certain outside influences. The nurses at the hospital had, for example, a habit of developing "crushes" of a kind on leading surgeons. You took a nurse out for a walk and she spent the time talking about Dr. X or Dr. Y and about what a "smooth" operator he was—how he could take out an appendix in eight minutes and how you had to be on your toes when you "scrubbed" for him. On and on and on! This counted, especially as the nurse was usually pretty and attractive. Moreover, the moving pictures had discovered the dramatic possibilities of the operating room and were exploiting them to the full. It was no wonder that we talked and dreamed about nothing else except specializing in surgery. There were a few students among us who had money enough to enable them to take an unlimited number of post-graduate courses and so in time become specialists, but for most of us the only hope was to qualify for a surgical residency where we could do hack work for three to five years in a big hospital under well-known surgeons and in return get the necessary experience and training.

It was understood that the three or four men who came at the head of the list in the final-year examinations were in line for the special appointments, so in those last two years we burned our eyes out studying. The last year was the year of the real "rat-race"—a term used to describe the frantic competition to cram as much knowledge as possible in preparation for the final examinations It was a nightmare year in one sense, but there were compensations. For one thing we had living quarters in the hospital—a row of rooms in the basement—and we spent our days in the wards and in the operating rooms. It was a time of excitement and pride of accomplishment as we came to do the things of which we had been studying the theory for so long. I remember the day a surgeon first let me stand on the right side of the operating table and guided my overeager and unskilled hands in doing my first appendectomy. When I came downstairs that day I was the perfect version of the moving picture surgeon—sombre, thoughtful, and dramatic of countenance, walking and moving with a great affectation of calm.

It was during this time that I met the hazel-eyed Sally MacNeil. She had been scrub nurse at my first operation. She had seen me at work and had not ridiculed my efforts —which may have influenced me. At any rate, I began to see as much of her as my strenuous program would allow.

For all of us the year was marked by one event, or rather what should be called a change of thought. This came upon us I don't know how, but one week everybody was talking about specializing in general surgery, and the next week we knew that this was not the highest goal in the world. There were the super-specialties. We began now to talk of being thoracic surgeons, or plastic surgeons, or GI surgeons—meaning surgery of the gastro-intestinal tract. Almost overnight, the idea of being general surgeons became flat and mediocre.

As for me, I was going to be a brain surgeon.

Those blank, unexplored spaces in the diagrams of the brain had begun to obsess me, and it seemed that all my life had unknowingly been directed to this one end. I would not only help to fill in those wide empty areas in the diagrams, thus advancing the science to which I had dedicated myself, but I would belong to the highest caste in the surgical world.

This then was my secret ambition and for it I forsook much. I almost ruined my eyesight, my nerves and my general health in my efforts to come near first in class, which was my only chance, as I well knew that my parents could not possibly finance me in a program of independent study. They had already done more than enough.

About four months before examinations the blow fell which nearly strangled my ambition in its infancy. One day I received a summons from the office of the dean. I went over quite cheerfully, secretly expecting some commendation for my good work. The dean was a fine man— one who took his work and the interests of his students very much to heart. But when I walked into his office and saw his grave expression and the way he settled his tall frame into his chair as if bracing himself for some unpleasant duty, I knew something was wrong. He started the conversation abruptly.

"Doctor, you're killing yourself!"

I relaxed a little. "There's nothing wrong with my health, sir," I said. "A little tired perhaps, but that's all."

He shook his head. "More than a little, I think. And," he hesitated, "I dislike telling you this, but you're exhausting yourself for nothing. You have no chance of getting a residency. Even though you were to come highest in every subject, we still could not recommend you."

While I stared at him, too shocked to speak, he went on to explain that, while I'd done pretty well over the five-year course, half a dozen others had done better. The board could not, he told me, make recommendations for the much-sought-after residency positions on the results of final examinations alone; it was necessary to take many other factors into consideration.

"However, don't worry," he finished kindly. "After all, there is nothing we need more than good, sound general practitioners."

For the next two weeks I went around half in a stupor. I did my work on the wards, assisted at operations and worked on my books in the evening, in a desultory, indifferent way. I was in a bitter, foolish and selfish state of mind. It did not occur to me that thousands of young men would have given anything they possessed to be in my position.

Then I overheard a chief surgeon talking in the dressing room just off the main operating room.

"I have a good friend down in Hants County," Dr. Belter was saying, "a fine old fellow; sends me quite a few cases. Quite a character; owns a cranberry bog and talks about nothing but cranberries. Ha, ha! Eccentric, but knows his stuff just the same. Knows more about kids than I do and good OBS man. Tells me he does two hundred deliveries a year, and I believe him. Worth a lot of money. Told me in confidence that he does fifteen thousand a year! That and practically no overhead!"

I didn't hear any more. I didn't need to. Suddenly my thoughts had made an about face. If it were possible to make money like that as a GP, why, one might stand it for a year or two, make a good stake, and then go off to study any specialty he chose. Once the idea took hold, I wondered why I had not thought of it before. I could bear to be a "fine old fellow" for a couple of years, if, in the end, I could be a brilliant young brain surgeon!

From that moment on, I saw everything in a new light. I wondered how I could have been so cowardly as to be depressed about the little setback I had had. There was nothing to it. It would just mean a little interruption in my upward career. Besides, the extra experience gained as a "man in the field" would not be entirely wasted. It would be dull, of course, but I would make the best of it, and the two years would fly by pretty fast.

I set out at once to work out the details. The first thing to do was to pick the location in which I was to start practice. I got out a map of my native province and studied it. There were hundreds of small towns and villages and I went over them one by one, trying to pick out the place most suitable for my purpose. I made discreet inquiries among my fellow students and among some of my teachers whom I knew sufficiently well. But no one, it seemed, could give me much help. They named various localities of which they knew, but always the fact came out that these places were already well supplied with doctors or that the economic situation of the area was very bad. It was the year 1934 and the great depression, while it had started to lift in other parts of th   rld, still blanketed most of Canada.

Two months went by and still I was no nearer finding a solution. I began to get anxious. It would soon be graduation time and I still had not found a location, although I had but two in mind—my home town and the city of Halifax.

It was at this point that Fate, in the guise of the frail little man dressed in black, knocked at my door.

Chapter Two

THE road to Canso follows the coastline very closely. It goes up and down more than it goes from side to side. One moment your wheels are splashing the salt water and your windshield is whipped by a driving rain of ocean spray. The next you are climbing a narrow shelf of rock to a height of six or seven hundred feet and you are conscious that from the edge of the shelf there is a sheer drop to the rocks way down below. You must drive very slowly because the road is full of holes, and here and there are outcroppings of rock that threaten to tear out the undergear of your car.

As you go on, a curious phenomenon strikes the eye. Under the continuous drenching by salt spray and mist, there is a gradual fading out of color in the scenery. Mile by mile, the grass becomes less green. Huge granite boulders are strewn about in greater and greater profusion —left there from the age of glaciers. In the rocky soil the spruce trees noticeably turn gray and become smaller in height and thickness, grow warped and crooked and their branches on the side facing the sea are only dead sticks.

Now the dwellings become more shabby and devoid of paint and the distances between them longer and longer until at last you find yourself driving for miles in a world that is only rock, sea and sombre sky. The roar of heavy surf is in your ears and the smell of the Atlantic is in your nostrils.

About seven miles before you reach Canso, the road, no longer able to keep its perch on the cliffs, turns inland so that you approach the town from the rear, that is from the side away from the harbor.

On my first journey of exploration in July I had met a few people, among them a Mrs. Gary, widow of my predecessor who had died two years ago. From what she told me I was convinced that while one could never hope to become rich in Canso, a single man living economically should have little trouble over a two-year period in saving the amount of money I required. Furthermore I had found out that I really was wanted in Canso—as Dr. Thompson had said—and this had a considerable influence on me. After all, there were not too many towns in the world which even knew of my existence and in those few I was not aware that there was any great clamor for my services. Also, Mrs. Gary had offered to make things easy for me by letting me have a room in her household at a nominal rent, and the use of her late husband's office in the same building for no rent at all. This evidence of welcome, I think, clinched my decision.

Now, in August, I was making my second journey,

ready to begin work. I was driving a new Ford V-8, on which I had not made even a down payment, loaded with surgical instruments, drugs and equipment trustfully provided on credit by firms in faraway Toronto and I had a hundred dollars in my pocket that I had borrowed from the bank. Even the gasoline which drove me along was "on the books" of the man who had so obligingly sold me the car without money. Yet although every bite I ate, every mile I drove, every cigarette I smoked, everything I picked up and put down, was done with someone else's money which would have to be repaid at seven percent, I found I was worried less about this than about the way in which I would measure up to the responsibilities of the work ahead.

It may seem inconsistent that a man who is planning a career in brain surgery should worry about whether or not he will recognize a case of measles if he sees one, yet every doctor starting in practice feels like this. In later years he acquires more confidence in his ability to handle situations but he never—though he may have fifty years of experience—acquires certainty. The world-famous surgeon is still thankful when he ferrets out an appendix and finds that it is inflamed, and that therefore his diagnosis has been correct. A good doctor seldom claims to be absolutely sure of anything.

I arrived in Canso at about four o'clock in the afternoon. I did not go directly to Mrs. Gary's, for I wanted first to look over my domain. To many people I know it would seem the most desolate, barren, rocky, miserable place on earth. Most of the houses were only the poorest kind of shacks. The streets were either mud, or bare rock—a natural pavement made smooth by the action of centuries of ocean spray and wind. The main street, I saw, was crooked. About half of it was so close to the ocean that the small shops on that side rested on thick wooden piles sticking out of the water. There were long gaps between buildings and in these spaces you could see boats of various sizes. Some had been pulled up on land and rested on blocks, others were afloat and tied to the building supports. Small flimsy jetties fringed the shore, at each of which a dory or perhaps a larger boat was tied up. In some cases the jetty was also part of the foundation of the fisherman's cottage. Men were seated on upturned buckets repairing the netting of lobster traps and little children played around the boats or chased one another over the rocks. From the main street also you could look across the water and see the three islands which form the harbor and are therefore responsible for the very existence of the town.

For some reason I did not find it depressing. There was a certain fascination about the place and the scene which was to grow stronger in the months to come and was to keep me there long after I should have gone.

At one spot about halfway down Main Street, there was a group of twelve houses which seemed decidedly out of place, as if they belonged in a city suburb. These, I found later, were the homes of employees of the Western Union Cable Company, for transatlantic cables come ashore a few miles away and there is a relay station at Canso.

Mrs. Gary was a young woman of unusual charm, tact and patience. She had need to be patient because from the day of my arrival the peace of her home was to be shattered by a confusion of people coming and going at all hours and a perpetual ringing of telephone and doorbells. She must often in the following months have doubted her own wisdom in taking in such an irregular lodger, especially as she was paid so irregularly most of the time, but she did not show it. Her five-year-old daughter,

Mora, would zip through the house, bursting open and slamming shut four or five doors, with the fury of a small tornado. There were to be times when I felt like helping her fall off the end of a wharf. But she had a way with her for all that and most of the time I would not have drowned her in anything worse than chocolate ice-cream soda.

I had the best room in the house—on the side facing the harbor. The house was not quite near enough to the water's edge to allow me to fish from my bedroom window, but still it was close enough. I could watch the boats going to and fro, hear the thuck-thuck of the oarlocks—most of them were rowboats—and read the names painted on them. One was called the "Free-Love." I wondered what kind of man her owner might be. Directly across the harbor was the bald domelike island called Grassy Island. On it had stood, more than two hundred years before, a great fortress which had figured prominently in the war between the French and the English. There was nothing there now, not even a fisherman's shack, and not the smallest vestige of the once-proud citadel remained.

Before going to bed, I went through a small book on the history of Canso which Mrs. Gary had sent up to me. I read that John Paul Jones, famous hero of the American navy, had made a "dastardly and piratical raid" on Canso during the Revolutionary War. He had not injured any of the inhabitants but he had, according to this account, taken all the rum and dried fish in A. N. Whitman's store —an institution which stands to this day—and burned some ships belonging to King George. When I turned off the light in my room and looked out over the quiet moonlit harbor I could picture his black ship, the *Providence,* stealing in over the water. I could hear the cries of the terrified inhabitants in the street below me as they saw at the masthead the banner bearing the defiant words

"Don't Tread on Me." John Paul Jones was physically a small man, only five feet, seven inches tall, and moreover he had severe rheumatic heart disease. Yet he had had the temerity to wave that flag in the faces of all the Admirals of England! I wished I had some of his courage. I was going to need it.

I was still unpacking my equipment the next morning when I had my first patient. A woman of about thirty years of age, who looked as if she were forty, came to the office carrying a small, thin and sickly infant in her arms.

"I don't know what to do with him," she told me, with a wan and helpless expression. "He don't seem to be gaining any and he cries all the time."

"What kind of formula are you giving him?" I asked her.

"Formula!" she repeated in a puzzled tone.

"The milk," I said. "How much do you give him and how do you mix it?"

"We don't give him no milk at all." She obviously considered my question very odd. "After all he's four months old."

I looked at her in surprise. "You don't give him milk!" I exclaimed, "Why not? What do you give him then?"

"There ain't no milk," she answered. "There's not even one cow in Alewife Point where we live. You don't expect us to buy canned milk, do you?"

I did not know what to say, so I repeated, "Then what do you give him?"

"Fish, of course," she replied, "what else! Dry cod. I grate it up and he kind of chews it, although he ain't got any teeth yet, and swallows it. And of course he gets bread and molasses too. Molasses is very good for babies. Sometimes we give him a little tea."

"Fish and tea at four months?"

"Sure, the tea is strengthening. Sometimes I stir a little flour into the tea to give it body like. That's strengthening too and besides it makes the bones stick together good."

Fish and tea and flour for a baby of four months! I thought for a while and then I wrote out a formula for the baby consisting of evaporated milk, corn syrup and water. I also wrote a note and told her to take it to the store and give it to the storekeeper. She was not satisfied.

"Aren't you going to give him any medicine?" she asked.

"All the medicine he needs is proper food," I said, "and don't give him any more dry cod and tea."

She still looked doubtful but she went away.

This, I learned, was a pretty general way of feeding babies in many sections of the area. The reason for the lack of cows was the lack of fodder, for there was hardly space for grass to grow between the rocks. Some years before, goats had been introduced into the area with the idea that they might be able to thrive where cattle could not. But the goats had not flourished. The people had for so long been accustomed to taking their living from the sea that they did not readily learn anything pertaining to farming nor, with a few exceptions, were they interested. There is a point at which poverty takes away even the will to escape from poverty. Many of these people, I was shocked to find, had long ago reached this stage. My opinion of Dr. Thompson went up a few notches when I thought that at least he had tried to do something about it.

This first case had a curious sequel.

A week or so later I called in to see Alex Doran, the storekeeper to whom I had sent the woman. I asked him for the bill.

"Four eighty, Doc."

I paid him and then he said, "Do you know what happened to that case of milk?"

"No," I said, "but I hope the baby is drinking it. Why do you ask?"

"Oh, nothing," he said, "only the day after I gave them the case, she came in here and bought a new yellow scarf. One of those in that show case there, for a dollar and a half, and that's not all. That same afternoon, Pete Smith came in and offered to sell me a case of milk. Told me he'd take three dollars for it. I bought it—here it is here."

"You mean she sold the milk to Pete Smith and bought a new scarf!" I yelped.

"That's right, Doc." He looked at me shrewdly and then he laughed.

"Give it up, Doc," he said.

I found out later that the baby had recovered anyway. At least it survived. After I got over my first indignation at having been made the unwilling provider of a silk scarf, I reflected that perhaps the scarf had made the mother happy. Happiness is contagious, it is a magic medicine, better for many things than the very best to be found in a drugstore. Maybe that was why the baby had got well.

The afternoon of my first day was a busy one. An elderly man with a gnarled and weather-beaten face came in. He was not a person who believed in wasting words. He said abruptly, "Wantcher take a wen off me haid."

"Oh," I said, "I'll be glad to. Let me see it."

"Just a wen," he said. "Had lots of them taken off before. Blacksmith used to take them off for me."

I was surprised. I had never thought of a blacksmith as a possible rival in surgery. I looked at the round ball about the size of a walnut, on his head. I took the instruments I would need out of their case and put them into the sterilizer to boil. They were new and shiny. Somehow I had not pictured myself as using them to remove wens. The cyst I was about to remove was separated from the brain only by about a quarter inch of bony shell, but it might as well have been on his little toe for all the drama involved. For a moment I was almost sorry that wens were so innocent. Then I put the evil thought out of my mind. I got out iodine, novocaine and a syringe. The patient was eyeing me suspiciously.

"The blacksmith just used a pocketknife," he said, "and he didn't need to boil it on account of he used it to cut tobacco and tobacco is better than boiling to kill germs any day."

"It is?" I said, wondering whether he might not be right.

"Sure is," he replied.

I shaved the surrounding scalp, painted it with iodine and injected novocaine. Then I made a small incision and the wen, which is a cyst or bag filled with cheesy material, popped out. I put in two sutures. Including the time spent in boiling the instruments, the whole procedure took about half an hour. He thought I was making an undue ceremony of it. The blacksmith, he said, used to do the whole job in less than five minutes. When he left I was a little let down. I wondered how many other things the blacksmith could do.

The next patient was a young man about twenty years old. He looked as though he might be a little bit defective mentally. He had a bad headache, he said, but he did not give the appearance of suffering very much. I asked him how long he had had it.

"About an hour," he answered. I knew then that there was nothing wrong with him that I could cure, but I decided I would have to examine him anyway. I found him physically perfect, told him so, and gave him a dozen tablets which, I explained, were simply aspirin tablets.

"How much is that?" he asked me.

"That will be two dollars," I told him.

He looked down at the floor and then he said, "You better take these tablets back, Doctor. Two dollars is too much to pay for a dozen aspirin tablets."

I knew it would be useless to try to explain to him. "All right, never mind it."

As he was going out the door, he turned and said, "I ain't got any money today, Doctor, but as soon as I get some I'll come back and give you a quarter for the tablets."

"Never mind," I said.

"Sure, I will, Doctor. Don't you worry. You'll get that quarter."

After this depressing interview I was glad to see that the next patient was a bright, pleasant-faced young woman. She had two children with her. The children had the itch, she explained to me, and she wanted some medicine for them. I reflected that I had been wasting my time when I worried about whether or not I would be able to make diagnoses. They were being made for me. I examined the children and found that the condition actually was scabies, or "itch" as it is commonly called, and I gave her a supply of a suitable liquid preparation, with careful instructions as to the method of using it. When I had finished she told me that the children had had the condition for quite a long time. She said she was anxious to get it cleared up as soon as possible, because she was going to be married in two days' time and she wanted the children to look as nice as possible and not to be scratching when she brought her new husband home.

"Oh," I said, "how long have you been a widow?"

"I'm not a widow," she replied laughing cheerfully and

entirely without embarrassment. "The fathers of these two children are living all right."

"Fathers?" I said, trying not to look surprised. "You mean they have different fathers?"

"Of course!" she said in an amused voice one might use to a child. "The father of this one"—she indicated the elder, a boy of about five—"was Alex Nichols. He was on a boat from Gloucester, and talk about a nice man! He was a real swell guy. We would have got married only he has a wife and two children in Gloucester." I was speechless. "The father of this one," she went on, pointing to the younger of the two, "is Jimmy Peet. He was on a boat from New Bedford. He's a real nice guy too, but kind of slow and dumb in some ways."

"Is he the man you're going to marry?" I asked, fascinated by this frank and unabashed autobiography.

She gave me a look of reproach. "Me marry Jimmy Peet! I should say not! He's not my type. Besides, his wife is sick and I don't believe in taking a man away from a woman that's sick. I believe in being square. I'm going to marry Jerry Flynn. He owns his own boat, a twenty-four footer, and he has a man working for him that he pays regular wages. He's a swell guy too." She went out smiling cheerfully.

Before I had time to digest this amazing conversation another patient came in.

This was a tall, raw-boned young fisherman with a wholesome, rugged face. He held out both wrists, a brass chain wound around each. "The salt-rheum," he said. "The chains don't keep it off, although I wear them all the time."

His wrists were covered with a purplish eruption and looked raw and sore. I had never seen anything quite like it before, although later it was to become very familiar.

It apparently occurs from the chafing of the wrists by the edges of sleeves of oilskins or rubber coats wet with sea water. I gave him some ammoniated mercury ointment and told him to use it three times a day. I also told him to be sure to report to me if the condition did not clear up in a few days. I later learned that it had, and I also found in the course of time that the brass chains, which were worn by nearly all the fishermen, actually were of some help in preventing the trouble.

All that first afternoon and late into the evening there was a steady stream of patients. About two thirds of them came with minor complaints. The remaining third were people with more serious troubles. For most of them I was able to do something. In addition to the office work I made some four or five house calls that day. At half past ten that night I sat down to rest and think over the day's activities. I was very pleased with myself and paid no attention at all to the fact that for this busy day's work I had received in cash exactly two dollars.

Chapter Three

As THE weeks went by, I began to gain more confidence in my ability to diagnose and treat the endless variety of illnesses that confronted me. I found I had been trained better than I thought. Of course I had to resort often to my books—French's *Differential Diagnosis*, and Beckman's *Index of Treatment* were my standbys—and sometimes to the long distance telephone by which I got in touch with my old professors when I was puzzled. Anyway I managed. The jangling of the telephone bell no longer sounded to me like a signal to "go over the top."

But another imp remained to torment me. Somewhere in my brain he lurked and kept whispering to me over and over that, no matter what I did, somebody else somewhere could do it better. If I opened an abscessed hand, he told me that my professor of surgery in Halifax would have done it more skillfully and more easily. When I delivered a new baby, he pointed out faults in my technique and suggested that if De Lee in Chicago could see me he would sneer with contempt. I never met Dr. De Lee although I am very well acquainted with his books on obstetrics. I wonder if he ever sneered. The fact that my patients consistently did well under my management did not help very much. I continued to go around with the uncomfortable feeling that while my patients were expecting the best, they were not getting it.

This feeling had a very concrete result. The great majority of the people for whom I did things did not pay me. With some it was because they were unable, but with a great many it was simply because it was inconvenient. I was very conscious of the fact that I needed to make money, yet I did not have the heart to urge these people to pay. An impersonal observer might have said this was charity on my part. He would have been wrong. I lay claim to a few charitable acts of course, but the angel of brotherly love deserves less credit for my good deeds than my invisible imp with his constant reminders that the Mayo brothers were better doctors than I. I longed for the time when I could begin to study my chosen specialty. It seemed to me that if I were doing only one thing, no matter how complex that might be, I could in time master it and in consequence, be able to hold up my head in pride.

Meanwhile, the foreseeable future held only long calls over rough roads in the dead of night, no money, little thanks, and not even the sense of satisfaction that normally should accompany the doing of a good deed for somebody in trouble.

The hopeless poverty of most of my patients probably

was as effective in depressing my spirits as in keeping my pockets flat. There were the Ben Felters, for instance.

I got home one day to find another call waiting for me: a baby was sick at Ben Felter's. Besides Ben and his wife, in the two-room shanty lived Ben's aged father and mother, and eight children. The entire family, with a couple of neighbors from the house next door, were crowded into the kitchen when I came in. In spite of the number of people, there was dead silence, as the father pointed to a crib.

I had delivered the baby two days before, but now it was dead and seemed to have been dead for several hours. I touched it and the body was cold. I asked some questions and it struck me that the answers came hesitantly and rather vaguely. They had found the baby dead, two hours before calling me. I asked them why they had not called me at once. They only looked at me in dumb and uneasy fashion. Finally Ben spoke up hesitatingly, "We didn't like to bother you. We know you're busy."

This was not true of course. Like some of their neighbors, they were people who did not hesitate to call me at any time for the most trivial matter. They knew it did not cost anything to call a doctor because they had no money with which to pay.

"It wasn't a strong baby ever since it was born," the father added.

I looked around at them, especially at the mother, a wan-looking creature, sitting near the stove, her face expressionless. The old grandmother was rocking to and fro in a corner looking at the floor and mumbling to herself. Then I remembered something. When the baby was born we found it had a cleft palate. It did not breathe at once and I had had a little trouble. I remembered the old woman had said at the time, "It'd be a blessing if God would take him."

This kind of remark is common enough, and I paid no attention to it. But now, looking at the feather pillow which lay alongside the crib, I wondered. I went over to the old woman, and asked her to come outside and talk to me. When we were a little distance from the door I asked her if she had any idea of what could be the cause of the baby's death.

She did not look at me but kept staring down at the ground and mumbling to herself. I could make out only a few words repeated over and over: "God forgive me. God forgive me."

I did not ask any more questions. I went home and a few days later when they came around with a death certificate to be signed, I wrote down as the cause of death "Broncho-pneumonia."

Aspiration pneumonia is common in babies who have a cleft palate. Regurgitated food is inhaled into the lungs and a broncho-pneumonia is set up or perhaps even atelectasis occurs—which means collapse of a portion of a lung due to complete blocking of a bronchial tube. I was sure that this explained the baby's death. Was there a slight lingering doubt in my mind? Perhaps. At first I did some wrestling with my conscience. Then I became ashamed of myself for even faintly suspecting the grandmother. After all, she was nearly ninety. Moreover, there were eight children in that little house—children who chewed dry cod all day long instead of having proper meals, who were dressed in rags, whose shoes were full of holes and who wore no socks at all, even in winter when the thermometer dropped to fifteen or twenty below zero, and to whom a single orange and half a dozen hazel nuts wrapped in a piece of old newspaper made Christmas a ter-

rific occasion. Of course this baby had died of broncho-
pneumonia. What else! I know it was not my business to
usurp the powers of judge and jury, but neither was it my
business to introduce the police into this scene of abject
poverty and ignorance on the strength of so slight a
suspicion.

Did I falsify this death certificate? No. The law does
not allow a physician to say, "I do not know," in answer
to the question: "What was the cause of death?" Neither
can he say, "I think," or "Probably." Yet in many cases
he does not know. This applies to the men in large medical centers as well as to the general practitioners out in the
field. Contrary to popular opinion an autopsy does not
always give the cause of death. An autopsy carefully done
by a good pathologist will reveal the answer in a high
proportion of cases, but not in all. Moreover, even in very
good institutions not all autopsies are carefully done. It
may take hours to do even a superficial one. If the case is
obscure and tissues have to be examined microscopically
it may take days. There are not enough skilled patholo-
gists in the majority of hospitals to begin to do justice to
the work that should be done at times. Therefore the
vital statistics which are quoted so glibly in speeches and
slogans—"One out of every thirteen Americans will die of
X disease"—are not to be taken too seriously from the
point of view of accuracy. It is unfortunate that, in putting on drives for funds for research in various diseases,
these inaccurate statements should be used. Advertising
agencies are often employed in these drives and the man
who composed the striking slogan I have quoted may be
the same one who tells you that somebody's cigarettes have
been proven in a nation-wide survey to be good for your
throat.

Statistics lie and lie and lie. The fact that the drive is

for a good cause does not justify sweeping statements. The end does not justify the means.

Winter came. Snow covered the ground making it more beautiful to the eye, and bitter winds followed to howl around the queer stovepipe chimneys and whistle through the cracks and crevices of the flimsy shacks. For most of the people coal was as impossible to get as diamonds. They depended, as the majority of rural dwellers do, on wood for fuel. But here there were at hand no forests of thick spruce and pine. Many of the fishermen had to walk for miles to places where trees grew that were stunted and no bigger around than a woman's wrist. These miserable sticks they cut down and loaded on small sleds designed to be drawn by hand, or by one or two dogs. The dogs were not the fine huskies used in Alaska and the Yukon, but untrained mongrel animals of any shape or size. I knew of only four horses in the district and three of them belonged to the mail driver. With these four horses I became well acquainted during the winter.

Jimmy Mack, the man who drove the mail from Canso to Guysboro, took me on many of my trips when he could do so without interfering with his duties to the post-office department. His horses were big and long legged so that even if they could not run much, they could walk fast—on an average, five miles an hour—so that a short journey of seven or ten miles with them was not too intolerable. The other horse belonged to Johnny Hall and this poor animal took me on my longest and meanest trips. Brown, with no white markings at all, he was thin and wiry and too light for really hard work, but he had great courage and determination. I used to feel sorry for him. I feel sorry for most horses. They are among the most misused of domestic animals. Theirs is a life of all work and no play and, at best, terminated by a bullet. If God treated us as badly as we treat animals, such things as wars would be Sunday picnics by comparison.

It was fifteen below zero one evening when, just at dusk, Johnny Hall and I climbed into his open sleigh and started out for White Harbour, thirty-five miles and ten hours away. Fifteen below zero, in a place near the sea, is very cold indeed. We both wore fur coats and were dressed as warmly as we could manage, but were not equipped like those people who inhabit the extreme north and who have to contend with the severest climate nine months of the year. After the first hour out, we felt that the expression "chilled to the bone" had a very literal meaning. I could picture little crystals of ice in my spinal fluid. I said to Johnny, "Is it possible to get any colder than this!"

"Sure is cold," he answered. He was a good man, but not one to talk much.

During the next two hours we tried getting out and walking up the hills. This helped a little, but could not be kept up for long because of the slippery ice in some places and the heavy snow in others. Moreover, after the exertion of walking we seemed to be colder than ever as soon as we sat in the sleigh again. At long intervals there was an occasional small hut where we could have stopped to get warm and we thought of doing so, but by now it was pitch-dark and the people had already gone to bed. There was nothing to do but sit there watching the horse take one weary step after another.

During the last two hours both of us, I think, were a little delirious from the cold. I cursed the day when I had taken up the study of medicine. I thought of all the other occupations in which a man could engage, in which the hours were regular and he could work in comfortable surroundings, and be warm all the time. I remember having bitter thoughts too, about the patient we were going to see. There would be nothing wrong with him except a slight cold. He was probably sitting up at this very minute alongside a hot stove, drinking rum and hot water and laughing to himself at how he was making a fool of the new doctor. He would, of course, not pay me—almost no one ever did on these trips even though they might have the money cached in a tin box under the bed—but would promise to pay as soon as his cheque came in. Everyone, I had already found, was always expecting a cheque from somewhere or other soon. It was with this imaginary currency that I was paid nine tenths of the time. The real dollars were kept for more important uses than paying a doctor. All of a sudden, with all my heart I hated this patient whom I had never seen. I hated the country and I hated my own profession most of all.

Finally we arrived at the small house where the patient lay. As soon as I saw him, I forgot all about hating him. He was a very sick man and he was in extreme pain. I knew what was wrong with him before I got near the bed and before I heard a word of his story. He had acute urinary retention. There are very few conditions that can be more distressing than this. Also it can usually be very quickly and easily relieved. I gave the instruments I would need to a woman to boil for me and then I huddled over the stove in an attempt to get warm so that I could use them. The woman gave us hot tea and after a little while I began to get thawed out.

Sterilizing the instruments took about twenty minutes and all the time the man on the bed was writhing and moaning aloud. Normally with a patient suffering like this I would have been satisfied with less than twenty minutes of sterilizing time, but in this case I was so cold that I could not begin to help him until my hands at least became warm enough to move. Finally everything was ready and I started on the procedure that I expected would be so easy and so quickly effective.

I had no sooner started when I realized that I was due for trouble. Ten, twenty and then thirty minutes passed and I could make no progress. The poor man was in despair. He told me, between spasms of pain, that a year before the same thing had happened. He had then been rushed to the hospital seventy-five miles away. They had done a suprapubic cystotomy on him—made an opening into the bladder through the lower abdominal wall. They were to have done the second stage of the operation, which would have resulted in permanent cure, about two weeks later. During the two week interval, being free of pain, he decided he had had enough of surgery and in spite of every effort to persuade him to remain he had insisted on leaving the hospital without having the second stage done. Now, of course, he regretted his stubbornness. Getting him to a hospital was out of the question. The only thing that remained was to operate on him at once, just where he lay. I told him so and he agreed. He had so much pain that he would have let me cut off both legs if it had been necessary.

I took more instruments out of my bag and laid them out on the table. Not very many would be needed. We put them on to boil. The man's wife got out some towels and some clean cotton rags. These we scorched on the top of the kitchen stove until they were brown. I put out alcohol and iodine and broke open the suture tubes. It was not hard to decide on the anaesthetic. Ether was out of the question because of the oil lamps which were the only source of light, chloroform could not be handled safely by the wife or by Johnny Hall, but luckily I had novocaine.

This operation, although it involves a three-inch incision through the lower part of the abdomen, is a simple one and it did not take long to do. In a little while the wound was closed with the rubber drain securely in place and a big pad of cotton dressings over it, taped down with adhesive. The transformation in the patient was something to see. He actually cried with relief and joy, and in a little while he was sleeping the quiet sleep of exhaustion.

The woman gave me another cup of hot tea. As I drank it and smoked a cigarette I thought, "So what if I get paid with an imaginary cheque, and if I have to pay Johnny Hall with real and not imaginary dollars, and if there are lots of comfortable easy jobs with regular hours! This is worth doing!"

The glow of self-satisfaction lasted for about two hours on the trip home. Then it disappeared, of course, but something remained. I had a sense of lightness—as if I had got rid of some heavy and undesirable burden. At first I was not sure of what it was. Then I knew—my imp had gone! He had been chased away by a reflection that came to me as I watched the monotonous step of the brown horse and listened to the continued creak of sleigh runners over snow that was too cold to be slippery. The Mayo brothers with all their skill and all the facilities at their command could not have done what I had done for this man. They were in Minnesota two or three thousand miles away, and I was here. They and De Lee and Pollak and all those other great men might as well have been on the moon, as far as the people of Canso were concerned. Somehow I had overlooked this simple fact.

From that moment on I was happier in my work. I realized later that a cousin of the imp—a distant one—remained. He is with me to this day, but he is a pretty mild and harmless one. In fact I am kind of glad to have him. I think he does me good. At least he has saved me from a few falls.

Chapter Four

I WAS in Canso several months before I heard about Mrs. Norwell. Mrs. Gary told me about her one evening at suppertime. At least she told me what she knew of the weird story and made me curious to know the whole of it.

Mrs. Norwell knew that she was the only living person in the village of Marville Harbour. Now Marville Harbour was a small community of some twenty-five or thirty homes. It had a church and a store and a government wharf from which a ferry—a small gasoline launch—went back and forth across the bay to Lappville. The ferry belonged to Mrs. Norwell's great-grandaunt, a very old lady who lived with Mrs. Norwell. Or rather Mrs. Norwell and her husband lived in the home of the old lady. The great-grandaunt and the husband, and all the people who went in and out of the store and the church and the houses and all the people who crossed on the ferry were, Mrs. Norwell knew, only spirits. They were not real. She alone was real. She went to the store and bought groceries from a ghost storekeeper. She went to church and listened to a sermon from a ghost priest and afterward, on the way home, she chatted with some of her ghost neighbors who happened to be going her way. In her conversation with her neighbors she often used to say, in talking about ordinary domestic problems, "Of course, it's different with you because you are spirits, it's so much harder for a real person like me." Or "You have no idea what it's like, being the only person alive in a town; really, you ghosts have no idea!"

Marville Harbour was about forty miles away, at about the outer limit of my district. The doctor from Guysboro, about thirty-five miles away, used to visit the place more often than I did. But one day an emergency call came in. There had been an accident. Mrs. Bostick—Mrs. Norwell's great-grandaunt—had been badly injured. The voice on the telephone asked me to come just as quickly as possible.

When I arrived I found that Mrs. Bostick had fallen out of bed, struck hear head against a radiator and had a bad scalp wound. There was a lot of blood around, as with any scalp wound, but the old lady's condition did not seem to be too bad. The bleeding of course had stopped long before I arrived on the scene. Mrs. Bostick was a very old woman and she had been bedridden for a long time. Age had dulled her intellect but she was still rational and on occasion, I was told, could show by a sharp display of temper that she still considered herself very much a part of this world and of its doings. I sutured her scalp, put on a good dressing and finally left her quite comfortable.

Mr. Norwell had met me at the door and taken me up to see the patient, but when we came down, I met his wife. She was a middle-aged woman with white hair, of medium height, inclined to be a little stout, and I could see that she once must have been attractive. She had a rapt worried expression on her face. I said to her, "I think Mrs. Bostick will get better. The wound looks worse than it actually is. Naturally she is quite old, but I think she will get along pretty well."

"Of course she will get better," Mrs. Norwell replied. "She can't die since she is a ghost."

I was trying to think of some way of getting her to talk about herself, when she solved the problem for me by asking, "I wonder if you would take my blood pressure for me while you're here, Doctor. I used to have high blood pressure."

That was my cue. While I was taking her blood pressure, I began to ask her questions. She was very willing to talk and I spent more than an hour with her. I did not refer to her "ghosts," but I led her to tell me about her past, her background. I learned a good deal of the story and when I left I resolved that I would learn more on my next visit. I made two other visits after that during which I spent much more time with Mrs. Norwell than I did with the old lady. Old Mrs. Bostick got better, and Mrs. Norwell . . . I will tell what happened to Mrs. Norwell at the end of the account which I have put down here. The arrangement of the story is mine; Mrs. Norwell gave it to me in more fragmentary fashion.

Once upon a time there was a pretty young girl who worked in a chocolate factory in the city of Boston. She roomed with three other girls in a small apartment over a Chinese restaurant in Hanover Street. She was in love with a good-looking, smart young man who worked for the tramcar company. If any reader wants to laugh at the chocolate factory-tramcar background for romance, let him. It shows he hasn't lived long enough or has seen too many moving pictures. Anyway these two were very much in love. They used to meet every night at a little restaurant called the Golden Hours, where you could eat for fifteen cents and drink beer for five cents, and which was so tiny and so noisy with other girls and young men that they could be absolutely by themselves.

They were very anxious to be married. They talked about it all the time and planned for a wedding to take place as soon as their combined earnings totaled eighteen dollars a week. How they fixed on this figure, I do not know. They knew their romance was something special and out of the ordinary and that they must not be married in the poverty of sixteen dollars a week which was what they were now earning. At this time she was twenty years old and he was twenty-four. Time went on without any raises in the pay envelopes and the first thing they knew, she had reached the mature age of twenty-one, and he of twenty-five, and still they were no nearer the fulfillment of their dream.

One day something wonderful happened. A letter came from the far-off country of Nova Scotia. When Celeste— that was the girl's name—read this letter, she danced and jumped for joy. She could hardly wait to break the good news to John and she looked forward with great eagerness to the evening when he would call for her.

Then the instinct for drama caught her and she planned how to break the news to him with the greatest effect; because this was no ordinary news—it was something out of a story book. Her mind flashed in a dozen different directions at once. First, she must buy, at once, the dress in the window uptown which she had passed by and admired so many times. John would be astounded when he saw her in the new dress, with her hair fixed up and everything. She would wear an air of mystery and refuse to tell him anything until they were in their favorite nook in the Golden Hours. Then she would make the dramatic announcement.

John arrived at the appointed hour and he was impressed indeed—not by the dress, which he hardly noticed —but by the air of mystery which was certainly very obvious. He coaxed her to tell him what it was all about, but she refused to say anything except "you just wait and see." She even contrived to tantalize him on the way by talking about ordinary things not related to the subject, and she felt very sophisticated in doing so. But once they were settled in the noisy little restaurant and their glasses of beer were in front of them and she had taken her first sip, she looked up at him with shining eyes and said, "What would you say, John, if I told you that I'm an heiress!"

"I'd say you were crazy, that's all. Say, what is this?" In answer she reached into the bosom of her dress and took out the letter.

"Here," she said, "read this."

He took the letter wonderingly, opened it and read.

Miss Celeste Peters
—— Hanover Street,
Boston, Mass.
My Dear Miss Celeste:
I am writing to you on behalf of your great-grandaunt, whom you have never met, but who is one of my oldest and best-loved parishioners. She is eighty years old and last week she fell and broke her hip. The doctors say they cannot fix

her hip because of her age. They also say she cannot last more than a few weeks because she will get static pneumonia and die. Also her kidneys are bad and her heart is none too good.

The neighbors are doing all they can for her, but your grandaunt is proud and sometimes she is a little difficult perhaps. She wants you to come and take care of her in her last illness because she says she wants someone to leave her money to, and you are her only relative that she knows of. I know that she has five thousand dollars ($5,000) in the bank in Wiseboro and perhaps a little more and besides she owns the ferry here, which brings in a good little sum. She wants me to tell you that if you come and take care of her all this will be yours and the house too, when she dies. She does not know that she will be dead in only a few weeks so, if you can, try to come quickly so that you will see her and bring her comfort in her last hours. Please wire me when you will come.

> Yours sincerely,
> —— P.P.
> Marville Harbour, N.S.

"Five thousand dollars!" said John slowly, a look of awe on his face.

"And a ferry and a house that we can sell for Lord knows how much besides!" Celeste said with a little squeal.

"Now we can do anything we want. We could open a restaurant, just like you always said you wanted to do—a place like this. Why, with all that money we could even buy this place if we wanted to."

They looked at each other in stunned realization.

"We must be married right away," she said, "and go together."

They sent a telegram and they were married and they started off for faraway Marville Harbour, to soothe the aunt's few remaining days and collect the legacy and have a honeymoon and live happily ever after.

When they arrived they found the aunt as frail and helpless as she had been described. She duly confirmed the promise that the priest had told them about in his letter. Celeste was a good-hearted girl and determined that she would carry out her part of the bargain as faithfully as possible. So she carried trays, and brought medicine and ran upstairs with drinks of water and made the bed—this was a difficult thing even for a strong young girl because the old lady would cry out in pain when she was moved even a little—and did all the things that have to be done for an invalid.

Weeks went by and the old lady received the best of care and all the neighbors spoke well of the young couple from the big city who were doing such a good job of taking care of the old aunt. When, at the end of a month, the old lady was still living, they all said it was due to the good care she was getting. While Celeste was busy in the house, John spent most of his time working about the small farm; cutting wood, looking after the hens and the one cow and so on.

Months went by, and then a year. The old lady looked as frail and helpless as ever but she did not get any worse except that she complained more and Celeste had to jump out of bed more often during the night in answer to her calls. At the end of the year, both she and John began to feel that they had fully earned the prospective legacy, and the five thousand dollars began to look rather small. But they comforted themselves with the thought that it would not be for very much longer.

Five years went by. The old lady was now eighty-six, very frail but still complaining, still demanding. Celeste was twenty-seven and John thirty-two. Celeste was not quite so pretty and she had lost her gaiety. John, too, no longer looked like a smart ambitious young man. He had to stay about the house almost all the time because Celeste could not handle the old lady alone. They would gladly have left everything and relinquished all claim to the five thousand dollars—which was still intact because the income from the ferry paid the day-to-day bills—but no one would undertake to look after the old lady for them at any price, and besides they were always conscious of the fact that any day she might contract pneumonia or take a stroke or something. When they were desperate and almost on the point of breaking away the thought would come to them that after all their work Mrs. Bostick might die the week after they left and someone else would get the reward which had already cost them so much in work and sacrifice.

Ten more years passed.

The old lady had turned ninety-six, Celeste was thirty-seven and John was forty-one. They lived month in and month out in a smoldering hatred of the aunt, the whole village, the whole province and the whole country of Canada, and almost, but not quite, of each other. They almost never spoke. The neighbors never came to visit now. Only the priest and the doctor came from time to time. They hated the doctor although his medicine had little or no effect in prolonging the seemingly useless life.

One evening something happened. Celeste was making her twentieth or thirtieth trip of the day into the old lady's bedroom. She sat on the edge of the bed and prepared to feed her patient from a bowl of vegetable soup.

Her aunt was in an especially disagreeable mood. Celeste had delayed an hour or two in changing her sheets; and moreover she had not seemed sufficiently repentant when reproached with this cruel neglect. All afternoon Mrs. Bostick brooded over this and by nightfall she had worked herself into quite a state. When Celeste was seated with the bowl of soup and just as she was dipping the spoon into it, two thin arms suddenly shot up and upset the bowl and its warm contents over her face and neck and down her dress. She jumped up and stood, shaking with anger, over the old woman. For one awful moment she thought she was going to strangle the old creature then and there, and her fingers curved. Then a curious feeling came over her. There was no need to strangle the old woman because she was already dead. It was only a ghost who lay there on the bed.

In a little while she came downstairs. John came in and she saw that he too was a ghost. From then on everybody was a ghost. The house was a phantom house. Nobody was real except herself, Celeste.

John got doctors who told him what he knew already—that his wife was suffering from a peculiar type of mental disorder. Someone suggested that he have her committed to a mental institution but he would not hear of this. In most ways Celeste acted naturally. Her delusion did not prevent her from continuing to look after the old lady as she had before. The doctors had, of course, advised rest, but she refused to rest. The doctors being ghosts as well, she did not have faith in them. In the course of time the neighbors who had flocked to the rescue when they heard of the dramatic illness, ceased to be excited by it and little by little the subject became commonplace. They accepted Celeste as she was, delusion and all. The only difference was that they were all kinder to her than they had been before.

When I encountered them the old lady was one hundred and four years old. She recovered from her scalp wound, but she died three months later. Celeste and John finally came into their inheritance. The five thousand dollars was still intact and they sold the ferry for three thousand dollars. So they had eight thousand dollars and a house.

Could a writer of fiction dare dream up a happy ending to this story? I doubt it. But here is the way it really did end.

Almost as soon as their burden had been lifted, Celeste began to get better. They bought a car and they took short trips. Little by little the delusion began to fade. She came back to the world of living people. She and John began to make plans. At first they thought they would go back to Boston. It had seemed such a desirable thing for them to do for all these years, but now, all of a sudden, the prospect did not seem so wonderful. But they took a trip there to look over the scenes of their youth. The Golden Hours Restaurant had disappeared but strangely enough they were able to find quite a number of their old acquaintances. The old friends all seemed to have taken a battering from the world. When John and Celeste told them of their experiences they were not very impressed, but related experiences of their own which they thought were even worse. None of them had eight thousand dollars in the bank, and those who owned houses had mortgages on them still. John and Celeste came away pitying them. They went back to Marville Harbour feeling quite cheerful. In time they converted the old house, which was very large, into a tourist home and had cabins for summer visitors who came to fish and hunt. They were successful. They had all the company they wanted and were as happy as two people could possibly be.

Chapter Five

ON THE morning of Christmas day, I had hardly finished breakfast when a boy came to the door to tell me I was wanted at his home at once as his mother was very sick. I knew the woman and I also knew that she was expecting a new baby. I groaned at my luck. If only the baby could have waited until Christmas was over! But as I was getting ready to go out with the boy, I reflected that after all it was still early in the day and, if I were lucky, I might still get back in time to have some kind of celebration. The boy said it was not very far away—only six miles —but he admitted we would have to walk part of the way as the road did not go right up to the house. I pictured a walk of perhaps a quarter to a half mile.

When we had covered not more than three miles with

the car the road ended abruptly. The boy explained that we would have to walk along the shore the rest of the way; his father would have met me here with the boat, but he had no gasoline. On a fine day in summer, I like nothing better than to walk along a rocky beach, watching the waves roll in, and looking in the crevices and hollows among the rocks for stray treasure carried in by the sea. But even then I would not enjoy three miles of clambering from one slippery rock to another. On a frosty day in winter it is most disagreeable and exhausting. The wind was cold, the rocks were cold and slippery and every now and then we were showered with icy spray. The boy wore rubber boots but I did not and before we had gone a third of the distance my feet were soaking wet. I hoped very earnestly to get the case finished and start back in time to make the return trip before dark. Even by daylight, it took almost two hours to cover the distance.

I had by now become quite accustomed to the sights of poverty but when I saw this house I realized that I had found a new low. The small rough dwelling was planted among the rocks just above the high-water mark, the side facing the sea whitened and encrusted with salt from ocean spray. It had been built to house fishing gear, nets, lobster traps, etc., then for one reason or another it had been abandoned, until a family like this one, so poor that they could not get a better place, moved in.

Inside was just one room. In the center was a large old cast-iron stove, obviously rescued from a scrap heap. There were also four beds, two against each side wall on opposite sides of the stove. At the end of the room opposite the door, stood a wooden table, and above that hung a couple of shelves on which were some dishes. That end, therefore, was the kitchen.

On one of the beds nearest the kitchen end of the room,

lay the sick woman. There were seven other people in the room, the husband and six children. The man was standing by the stove when I came in, poking wood into it, and the children, all dressed in outdoor clothes even to their caps, were seated on the edges of the bed. The man was an odd-looking person, with a long nose and eyes set very close together.

"Sure glad to see you, Doctor," he said when he saw me. "She's pretty sick."

I went over to the bed and talked to the woman. She told me she had been sick all night, but I knew at a glance that she was not telling the truth. She had sent for me with the very first pain, because she was nervous and frightened and there was no woman neighbor to stay with her. I did not say anything, but I asked her husband to get all the children outside for a few minutes so that I could examine her. When I had completed the examination I knew I was there for the day, unless I wanted to undertake a double journey over the three miles of slippery rocks. My heart went down in my boots, but there was nothing else to do. I was thankful I had brought along a good supply of cigarettes. I told the man that he could call the children back in out of the cold, then, picking out the cleaner of the two chairs I settled down to wait.

The children trooped in. With them was an older boy carrying a rifle and three birds, which he had apparently shot just a few minutes before. To my surprise, I saw that they were sea gulls. I had never heard of anyone shooting these birds before. They are protected, by law because they are useful as scavengers, and also by the fact that they are unpleasant to eat. Yet from the actions of the family and their conversation I knew that these gulls were going to be eaten—that, in fact, they constituted

Christmas dinner. The boy and his father had a brief argument about whether they should be plucked or skinned. They decided on skinning. I think if I had not been present they would have gone ahead with this operation right there in the room. As it was the boy took some necessary things from the "kitchen" and went outside with them. While he was gone, I looked around me. There was no sign of any other food in the house. When they started to prepare the meal I found that this was true. There was no bread, there were no potatoes, no butter, no sugar, not even molasses which was the standby of so many families in the area. There was a little tea. Sea gull and tea for Christmas dinner!

The boy came in with the birds, skinned and cleaned and each one chopped into four pieces, carrying them on a piece of board. His father took the board and spilled the meat into a pot which was half filled with boiling water. Then he put a lid on the pot and the cooking was under way. He came over and sat down near me.

I had been fingering a two dollar bill that lay in my pocket. What good would it do? I thought. Then I remembered that Mr. Bennet, the Baptist minister, had told me a short while before that he had been given a small amount of money to be used for needy families. I wondered if it were all gone, and decided to send him a note anyway. So I wrote a brief message telling him what I had found and asking him if there was any money left in the fund. Then I asked the biggest and strongest boy if he would deliver the note for me. He probably guessed what was in the note because he agreed with great eagerness and went off.

From observing and talking to the man and woman I judged that they both were mentally deficient. The woman, in between pains, smiled continually and talked and acted in general very much like a child. She did not talk much. She was not nervous or in the least concerned about anything, now that she saw I was here and meant to stay until everything was over. The man talked quite a lot. Our conversation ran something like this.

"You live quite a piece from the road," I said, "it must be kind of inconvenient."

"Yeah, sure is," he answered, "sure is."

"It must be bad for the children going to school," I said.

"Sure is, sure is."

"Are you able to do any fishing this time of the year?"

"No, not much, not much. Say, mind if I take one of your cigarettes?" I had left the package on the table.

"No, go ahead," I said.

"I sure like tailormades," he said. "They taste better."

Then out of a blue sky he added, "They's ghosts around here."

"Ghosts?"

"Sure, ghosts. You can hear them every night especially if it's stormy. I seen them once or twice."

"That's right," his wife chimed in, smiling. "I seen them, too. They was one looked like—" she broke off as a pain came on interrupting her thoughts. I reflected that in a place like this, at nighttime, with the wind howling and the spray beating down on the house and with only the dim light of a single lantern which was hanging from a nail in the wall, anyone could see a ghost.

An hour went by, and I judged it was time for me to think of getting my instruments boiled and putting things in readiness. The man found a pot and we put the instruments in it, covered them with hot water from the kettle, and poked up the fire. Another hour passed and I told him it was time for the children to go out for a walk. He bundled them out and I got my bottle of chloroform. I took the glass stopper out of it, inserted a little piece of string in the mouth of the bottle and reinserted the glass stopper. I tested the drip. The chloroform dripped evenly from the string wick, about two or three drops per second. I arranged the mask. Soon it was time and, with the pains, I started giving her the anaesthetic. Fifteen, twenty minutes, and then a half hour went by, and the baby was born.

Up to this point I had been going about my work in a rather weary and uninterested fashion. There is nothing particularly exciting about an obstetrical case when a patient is having her eighth baby. Moreover, I had been sitting in that dismal room doing nothing for the greater part of a day. My principal thought was to have everything over and done with, and start home to Mrs. Gary's comfortable living room, an easy chair, and a good dinner.

Suddenly I received a terrific jolt.

Before me was a thing of horrible deformity—what is known aptly, even in medical literature, as a monstrosity. It was the first I had seen outside of those in glass jars in the pathological laboratory at medical school. It had no neck and no well-defined head. Instead it had eyes and a mouth on top of what should have been its head. I cut the cord after tying it, watched the misshapen little chest move convulsively a couple of times, and then to my relief, all breathing stopped. I turned to the husband. He was staring in fascinated horror.

"Ghosts," he was muttering to himself. "I told you they was ghosts here. It's a devil-baby!"

"Stop that talk," I said sharply. "Hand me that towel, quickly. She's coming out of the anaesthetic."

He handed me a towel and I wrapped the baby in it.

"Now," I said, "she must not know about this. You

must not let her see it. Find a little box and tomorrow you will take it to the cemetery. I'll talk to the minister and you can just go there by yourself and bury it."

When the woman came back to consciousness I told her simply that the child was born dead.

"That's queer," she said, "I could feel it move right up till you gave me the ether."

She did not appear to be disturbed—only relieved that her ordeal was over. She was soon smiling cheerfully as ever. I turned to look at the man. He had an old shoe box, and he was tying string around it. He was using a lot of string and tying a lot of knots. I remember that the box was labeled at one end, "Elka Brand. The Shoe of Quality, Size 9½."

Such abnormal things are fortunately very rare. This is the only one I have ever seen in seventeen years of busy medical practice. What causes them? Nobody knows exactly. Some accident in development occurs at some time after the ovum and spermatozoon come together. Or even possibly there may be a defect in either one or the other of these exceedingly intricate cells before they are united. The sperm is so tiny that it can be seen only with a very powerful microscope. The ovum, or egg, is much larger than a sperm, but much smaller than the very finest grain of sand. Yet these two so very small particles contain within themselves patterns and designs for innumerable complex and wonderful things. There is a pattern for the heart—itself so intricate that an entire lifetime is inadequate for its proper study—a pattern for a brain, lungs, liver, spleen, kidneys, stomach, adrenal glands, pituitary glands, pancreas, arms, legs, eyes—all of them so complex —and yet the design for them is there in those two little cells. In these cells are written whether a man shall be tall or short, the color of his hair, the color of his eyes, the shape of his nose, the size of his mouth, the size of his muscles, whether he will be strong or weak. It is written also whether he will be clever or stupid, whether he will be good at mathematics or have a skill for poetry, whether he will love music—all the complex mechanism that makes a Paderewski or an Einstein is written here.

And the Pattern Maker! Where is He?

Just about the time I was leaving, my friend Mr. Bennet came into view. He was a very tall and very thin man, all arms and legs, and he came over the rocks like a spidery Santa Claus. In one hand he had a suitcase, and in the other a flour bag filled with good things. I doubted very much that there had been enough money left in the fund to supply all this, and reflected that probably the Bennet family would be on short rations for a while. I have met few characters more admirable than this man.

I waited outside until he had distributed his bounty. Then we started the walk back together. As we made our way over the icy rocks he was kind enough to say some good words about the work I was doing. But I am sorry to say I did not see things quite as he did.

"Let me get out of this and at my brain surgery," I thought. "I am no hero."

Chapter Six

IN ONE respect I had something in common with Harvey Cushing, Joslin, and all the other greats of the medical world—I worked as hard as they did, perhaps even more so. With some four thousand people in an area served by only one doctor. I used to see thirty or forty patients a day, drive an average of seventy-five miles and give advice by telephone twenty times a day.

All this activity left me little time and little inclination to think about the financial part of my affairs. I hated bookkeeping and figures and I did not have the type of mind for financial success. In college I had counted myself lucky because I had a father who was able and willing to finance my studies. I did not have to work my way through as did so many of my fellow students. Now it began to dawn on me, slowly and painfully that: a) money is necessary in this modern world; b) it is not so easily come by; and, finally, c) in the medical profession, unlike most occupations, doing much work may mean laying out money instead of taking it in.

After I had been in Canso about six months some small things began to occur which were slightly disagreeable. A letter came from the X and Y surgical supply company worded something like this:

> Dear Doctor:
>   Our draft for the sum of $197.67 was returned by the bank to-day, Dishonored. We are reluctant to take measures which must be unpleasant to you in this matter, but, unless you make a substantial reduction in this account within the next ten days we will be forced, against our wishes, to take some action.
>
>   Yours truly,
>   ——— ——
>   Acct. Dept.

I was not so sophisticated then as I later became and the word "dishonored" had a sting to it. In the same mail there was a letter from the automobile dealer which read something like this,

> Dear Doctor:
>   I am sorry to inform you that it will be absolutely necessary that you pay something at once on the car, which you know, we gave you in all good faith and trust on your note alone, saving you the big expense of dealing with a finance company. It is up to you now to do your part.
>   Will you please send two hundred dollars at

once and the rest in payments of at least fifty dollars each month.

Yours truly,

—— ——

I had visited the bank dozens of times in the past six months and had always regarded it as a very pleasant place. The manager and tellers and clerks were all genial good fellows who took pleasure in helping people. But today when I went in I had a slightly uneasy and half-guilty feeling. I said, "Hi, Ralph," and, "Hi, Joe," to the two tellers as I went by their cages. They said, "Hi, Doctor," perhaps in the same way as they always had, but I fancied I detected a little restraint in their manner. When I sat down in front of Mr. Kenny's desk, and looked at him, I was sure there was something wrong. I offered him a cigarette which he refused—he had never refused one before.

"Well, Doctor, what can I do for you today?" he said.

I had been going to say I wanted five hundred dollars, but when I began to talk the figures changed themselves in my mouth.

"Three hundred would do me today, Mr. Kenny," I said.

He tilted his chair back and put his hands behind his head, looking out the window at the same time.

"Your notes amount to eighteen hundred dollars now," he began, "and I have a letter from a certain automobile dealer who tells me he has a note of yours for nine hundred and sixty dollars on which you have not paid anything as yet. That makes twenty-seven hundred and sixty dollars—plus interest of course!"

"Well," I replied, "pretty soon now things will be better and—"

He did not let me finish.

"How much do you owe besides that twenty-seven hundred and sixty, Doctor?" he asked, fixing me with a cold eye. Suddenly my self-assurance began to weaken. I had no idea of exactly how much I owed. His manner rattled me. No one had spoken to me in that tone of voice since I was a boy in school.

"Perhaps four or five hundred," I said.

"There were drafts came through this bank for you in the last month alone to the amount of more than nine hundred dollars and you dishonored them all," he said.

The word "dishonored" is a common banking term used every day and which, perhaps, does not have its old-fashioned significance to people who are hard-headed businessmen; but to me it was a blow in the pit of the stomach. I got up, my face red, and without a word walked out of the office and into the street. Someone spoke to me as I went out, but I did not see or hear him. I got into my car and drove down to a place called Rockhead—a deserted beach about three miles from town. I was alone with the waves and the rocks.

If anyone thinks that the surest way to get into debt quickly is by riotous living, drinking and betting on horses, he is only partly right. There is just as certain a way and that is to be a doctor, work hard for eighteen hours a day, drive for miles over bad roads to see patients and give them expensive drugs. For a little while I felt sorry for myself. Then I spent a good half hour being angry at the bank manager and thinking of all the smart sarcastic things I should have said to him. Finally I got over this mood also, and began to wonder why it was that I could not collect money.

It was true the people were poor. Yet the liquor store in town supported three employees and their families and made a profit for the government besides. There was a motion picture theatre also, which ran shows two nights a week, and it made a profit. There were a half-dozen stores which had stood for a long time so they too must have been making a profit. And what about the three churches? True, I knew their clergymen lived meagrely, but at least they lived. The fault must lie with myself. I resolved that from that moment on I would be more strict about collecting money. I would revise my bookkeeping system and keep it right up to date. I would spend a half hour each night keeping my records in order. I went home stuffed full with firm resolutions.

I was still in this mood when, shortly before midnight, I got a call from a man named Matt Nichols who lived about twenty miles away. Someone was badly hurt at his place, he told me. Could I come as quickly as possible. Now here was a call I was tempted to refuse. I did not like Matt. A month before when I had slid my car into a ditch in front of his house, he had curtly refused to walk a hundred yards to help me, on the grounds that he was too busy mending lobster traps. Now he wanted me to drive twenty miles to his aid. He was notorious as a bully and a drunkard.

It was an ugly, foggy night but although I did not relish making the call, I thought the accident might really be serious and I decided to go.

In the fog it took almost two hours to get to the place. The house was a little off the road and as I drove into the front yard, I noticed that it was almost in darkness, with only a dim light coming from one room. I went to the door, knocked, and then walked in without waiting for anyone to answer. I knew they would all be drunk anyway. In the center of the room there was a table with a kerosene lamp on it. Alongside this table, Matt sat in a chair, very drunk indeed. Another man whom I recognized as Matt's brother was seated across from him in even worse condition and, lying on the floor, there was a third man, sleeping, whom I did not know. I first thought this man on the floor might be the patient but just then a woman came into the room carrying another oil lamp in her hand. She too was tipsy, but not to the same degree as the others. She was Matt's current "wife." She told me the injured man was upstairs.

I followed her up and found him lying there on a bed. There was blood all over the place—on the pillow, on the bedspread and on the floor. It was a mess. I examined him and found that in spite of all the gore his condition was not too bad. He had a long scalp wound and a portion of the scalp was detached from the bone and was turned back like a flap. There was no sign of a skull fracture. He had fallen down the stairs, I was told. Needless to say, he too, was very drunk but he was conscious and sober enough to struggle and curse when I tried to work on him.

The woman got me some warm water and I finally managed to clean the wound, shave the scalp about the wound edges, and get the edges well sutured together— while the patient struggled, cursed, and shouted that he wanted to be left alone to go to sleep. The woman could not help except for holding the lamp. When I had finished I applied a good dressing covering the whole top of his head. A dressing of this type requires care and takes five or ten minutes to apply properly. At last it was done and I gave the woman some directions. Then I went down to the room where I had first found the three men. I had my new resolution about getting paid fresh in mind.

When I came in, Matt stood up and said, "How is he, Doc?" He was very unsteady on his feet and kept one hand on the table to steady himself as he spoke to me.

"He'll be all right now," I replied and stood there waiting.

"Fine, fine," he said thickly, "certainly glad you could come out. Thanks a lot for coming, Doc."

He started as if to show me to the door. I stood still.

"That will be twenty-two dollars," I said.

Matt looked at me in surprise.

"Sure, Doc," he said after a moment. "I'll tell him in the morning when he sobers up, and he'll go in and pay you."

"No, that won't do," I said. "I want you to pay me; you and your brother and your friend here. You can pay me now."

Matt shook his head and began to look a little more alert.

"But he's the one that got hurt, Doc, it's none of my business."

"Look," I said, "the four of you and this woman have been having a drinking party together. You all get drunk and one of you gets hurt. It's up to all of you to chip in and pay me."

"Hey! You're crazy, Doc," said Matt slowly, "if you think we're going to pay you."

"All of you put your money on the table and I'll take my twenty-two dollars from the pile in equal shares from each." As I said this I kicked at the man on the floor gently to try to make him wake up.

"Like hell, we will," said Matt.

I have always been a very mild person; the kind that will not talk back to waitresses. The only real fighting I had done since my childhood days was at college—using gloves as big as pillows, and at that I was no champ. Before me was Matt, big and ugly and mean. Before I realized what I was doing I had smashed him a blow in the mouth that made the blood run and laid him out on the floor. His brother who had been sitting on the opposite side of the table, now got up with a wild look and started to lurch around towards me. I did not wait for him. I went after him. I had the advantage of being sober and also very angry. I caught him a good blow on the jaw that knocked him down. At the same time the woman, whom I had forgotten, screamed and dropped the lamp. The lamp shade broke and the flame blazed up as the oil began to leak out. There was a coat lying on the back of a chair. I picked it up and threw it over the lamp, putting it out.

The place was still lighted by the lamp which stood on the center of the table and I saw Matt getting up again. I hit him again before he was fairly up on his feet—I know it was against the Queensberry rules. This time he fell in a sitting position, his back against the wall. He was not unconscious but he did not try to get up at once. I looked around for someone else to hit. The third man, who had been lying on the floor in a drunken sleep, was awake and shaking his head in confusion. I went over to him and told him to get up off the floor, slapping his face a few times in order to emphasize the order. He got into a sitting position. Matt started to get up also, but not to fight. He reached into his pocket and threw a handful of bills on the table. Then, without a word, he went around the table to where his brother was lying and pulled him to his feet. He, too, emptied his pockets and put his money on the table. The third man did the same thing, with some assistance from Matt. There was more than a hundred and twenty dollars on the table. I took twenty-two dollars out of the pile and started to leave. As I turned, who should be standing in the doorway, staring stupidly, but the patient on whom I had been working only a short time before. He had ripped off the elaborate dressing I had fixed on his head and was holding it in his hand like a cap.

I said something to myself. I took him by the arm and made him sit in a chair. Then I seized the white dressing and pulled it over his head and proceeded to wind some three-inch adhesive tape over his head and under his jaw several times in such a way that not only would he be unable to get the bandage off without assistance, but he also would be unable to open his jaw. I told Matt to get him to bed and bring him to my office the next day.

I got into the car and started for home. The fog had lifted by now and the driving was easier. I thought, "What a dignified doctor I am! Getting into a fight with three drunks for the miserable sum of twenty-two dollars. How fine! How noble! What would my old professors at medical school think if they knew that I was collecting fees by means of assault and battery?" It was depressing. If just one of my victims had been sober I might at least have derived some primitive satisfaction out of the fight, but even this was denied me. It was an ugly episode. It was quite a long time before any of the humor of the situation struck me.

Needless to say I did not use this method of collecting bills again. It is not a recommended procedure for routine use. However, I stuck firm to my determination to pay more attention to the business part of my practice in the future. I must have succeeded, too, because, while I had gone in debt to the extent of three thousand, six hundred dollars in my first six months' of practice, during the next year I only went further into debt by an additional twelve hundred dollars; a total of four thousand, eight hundred dollars.

Fine progress I was making! Instead of nearing the goal which I had set for myself I was receding from it.

In spite of my good resolutions my bookkeeping system still depended to no inconsiderable degree on notations made on the back of cigarette packages—I remembered that I smoked Sweet Caporals at that time because the cardboard package was more suitable for writing than that of other brands—and on prescription blanks and other scraps of paper. Nevertheless when my debts had reached the four thousand level and I realized that I would now have to make nine thousand dollars instead of five before I could start on the plan I had outlined for myself, it dawned on me that sooner or later I would have to leave Canso.

Perhaps I would have recognized all this sooner had it not been for the fact that in spite of everything I was getting to love Canso and its people. The latter were continually surprising me. For example, the man who had been so roughly critical of my skill in removing wens was the same man who came after me with his motorboat one day when I was out rowing and a sudden storm came up threatening to blow me to sea. The young woman who had startled me with her frank account of her less than moral dealings with visiting seamen was also the one who shoveled snow with me on a twenty-degree-below zero day when my car was stalled not far from her house. Even Matt Nichols became a friend of mine in time. I came to appreciate Canso for its own sake—the smell of sea air, the sound of the waves, the haunting cry of the sea gulls, all contributed to create a sense of being in a world apart.

It may be that I would have remained there much longer and gone even more deeply into debt had it not been for a certain odd character who briefly entered my life.

One evening when I was finishing office hours, a stranger came in, a thin, stooped, shabby man. His clothes were old and thin and worn and did not fit him well. The coat was too large and his trousers were too small and he wore a bowler type hat. It was hard to tell from looking at him whether he was thirty or fifty years old. His face was lined and anxious and it was obvious that he was under great mental stress. What attracted my attention were his eyes —bright, quick and intelligent.

He said immediately, "Doc, give me a shot of morphine. I need it very badly. I know you don't know me, but I can pay, and I need it the worst way."

"Sit down," I said, "and tell me about yourself."

He sat down but immediately got up again and began pacing the room.

"I can't sit still," he said. "I'm an addict. I have to take three grains twice a day. I haven't had any this morning. Please, Doc, I can pay."

He paused and looked at me for a moment with the expression of a man pleading for his life, as, in a sense, he was. He began pacing the room again, from my desk to the examining table and then to the window and back again to my desk.

"Suppose you stop a minute," I said, "and tell me about it. I can't give you anything until I know some of the circumstances."

"Give it to me first, Doc," he said, "and I'll tell you all about it afterward. Right now, I can't think. I can hardly talk." He took a five dollar banknote from his pocket and held it out to me.

"I can't take your money," I said, "and it is against the law to give you morphine."

With this he started to plead again and then all of a sudden slumped down into a chair, put his two hands to his head and began to rock it back and forth. His eyes shut and his face went into a contortion of agony. I felt sorry for him. Perhaps a quarter grain would give him some relief.

"No more good to me than a drink of water," he said, "please let me have twelve tablets, Doc, please, please, please."

Suddenly he went down on his knees and began to wring his hands with an expression of despair. I was filled with embarrassment just looking at him—never before had I witnessed such a scene.

"Very well," I said, "here it is." I got out a tube of quarter-grain tablets and I was about to turn and get a hypodermic syringe, when he reached out as if to seize the tube from my hand. I pulled away and he stood still for a moment. Then I opened the tube and counted out twelve tablets. Immediately he went into feverish activity. He began to fumble in his pockets and to draw out a strange collection of objects. There was a medicine dropper, the kind with a little rubber bulb on one end, a hypodermic needle wrapped in a piece of old newspaper, and an old beer bottle cap from which the cork lining had been removed. I gave him the tablets and sat back to watch.

First he took the bottle cap and shook out from it the tobacco crumbs and the lint which it had gathered in his pocket. He then went over to the washstand and filled it with water. He put in the tablets, all twelve of them— enough to kill three ordinary men. Then, holding the cap between thumb and forefinger of his left hand, he lighted a match with his right hand and held the flame under it. When the match had burned down to his fingers he lighted another one and before the second was finished, the water had begun to simmer and the tablets had dissolved. He put out the match and set the bottle cap very carefully down on the corner of my desk. He did all this with an air of the greatest concentration, oblivious of me and of his surroundings, like a scientist conducting the critical phase of an experiment. Next he took the medicine dropper, made the needle fit by winding a strip of paper around the glass tip, and, then, by a series of squeezing movements on the rubber bulb, drew up every drop of the solution into this improvised syringe.

Now he performed what was to me a surprising feat. He took out a handkerchief, tied it around his upper left arm just above the elbow and knotted it securely, using his teeth instead of a hand in tying the knot. Then he began exploring the back of his wrist and hand. His left arm, all the way down to the wrist, was covered with tiny scars. Long ago the large veins had been obliterated by the repeated injections; then the smaller ones. Now he was searching the back of his hand for the smallest of veins. He found one that was almost invisible to me. He held the medicine dropper by the barrel between the thumb and forefinger of his right hand and placed the point of the needle just over the tiny blood vessel. He did not push or jab. Instead he began to spin the syringe back and forth with a drilling motion. I watched in rapt attention. He paused. A thin red column appeared in the glass tip. He bent his head with a quick motion and with his teeth loosened the tourniquet. Then skillfully and with great care, he manipulated the bulb until all the solution had been emptied into the vein. This accomplished, he scooped up all his poor implements and pushed them haphazardly into his pockets. Then he straightened up, looked at me and smiled.

I almost jumped in surprise. It was like a Hyde to Jekyll transformation. From a cringing wretched creature, in five seconds he changed to a poised, self-assured man of the world. Except for his clothes, he would have been able to take his place in almost any company. He talked in a cultured voice and in the manner of a person of some education. There was no sign of the mental exaltation or confusion that accompanies morphine intoxication. The huge dose he had taken was a minimum one for him. With it he became normal.

He told me a long story about his background and life before he became an addict, most of which I took with a grain of salt. This much, however, apparently was true. He had been taking morphine for twenty years. He had been in and out of a dozen institutions. On each occasion he had been weaned off the drug completely, but each time he had taken it up again as soon as he was discharged. While he had money he bought it through illegal sources at prices ranging from five to fifteen dollars a dose. When he had no money he was forced to go "on tour." That is, he toured the towns in a circuit a thousand miles long, from Portland, Maine, to Sydney, Nova Scotia. In each town he got a dose from one or more doctors—he could not be refused while he was in the state in which I found him—and then moved on to the next town. He was obliged to keep on the move continually, forced by this horrible hunger, except for the odd occasion when he came into a little money. Then he would hurry to the first city large enough to have narcotic peddlers—he knew them all —and stay there until his money was exhausted. These respites would never last for more than three or four days and then he would have to start the circuit once more.

When he was leaving my office he begged me for an extra dose for the next morning. I did not give it to him. If I had he would have been back the next day looking for another dose—a hopeless situation.

"I'll be back in about six months, Doc," he said.

"Don't come back," I replied. "The next time I won't be so soft." But I knew he would come.

Later on I had visits from two other addicts of this "circuit riding" type. I refused them both because I thought Cragg—as I called the first man—had told them about my helping him, and I did not want my office to become known as a way station for unfortunates of this kind. But I was sorry for them.

It is not true that all narcotic addicts are degenerates. Opium addicts have held positions of high responsibility in every walk of life. Often they have been among the leaders in their own trade or profession. They have ruled nations. The opium traffic itself—horrible as it now looks to us—was at one time a fairly respectable occupation. English merchants made fortunes in India, buying the drug and selling it to China. In fact when the Chinese government attempted to enforce a law prohibiting the entry of opium into that country, Britain went to war with China for the purpose of reopening the trade. This was in 1839—little more than a hundred years ago. The Chinese were defeated and actually had to pay for the opium they had destroyed! Furthermore, they were compelled to admit entry of the drug.

I knew at least one man who could be classified as a respectable opium eater. His case was particularly interesting to me for a couple of reasons. He was a man of about eighty, who had been a very prosperous business-man and when I knew him, he was, although retired from active business, still a person of considerable means. Forty-five years previously he had contracted the habit of taking laudanum, which is a solution of opium in alcohol and which was a drug in common use in those days.

Over a period of years he had gradually increased his

daily intake to the astounding amount of three ounces of laudanum a day. The standard therapeutic dose was twenty drops. He was taking enough in each twenty-four hours to kill twenty men. For a great many years he had had a special permit from the narcotics bureau so that he could purchase legally through a recognized drug house the large amount he required. He had also been in the habit for more than forty-five years of drinking one full quart of rum every day. He told me that when he was younger he took two quarts, but he may have been exaggerating.

Now it will seem strange that a man taking large quantities of liquor and opium for so long should be able to keep his health, keep his reason, and prosper in his business so as to become a comparatively wealthy man in the community. But he did all three. I have myself shivered at seeing him down an ounce of pure laudanum at a gulp, following it up with three ounces of rum diluted with only a very little water. But at the age of eighty he had the use of all his faculties, was bright, intelligent and an entertaining, even witty conversationalist. He was up to the minute on the current events of the day and knew a great deal about politics, international affairs and literature.

I can explain this only partly. He was, to begin with, a man of strong will who could refuse to take enough of either spirits or opium to render himself senseless. The quantities he took represented minimum doses for him, and did not affect his speech; his gait; nor, appreciably, his judgment, as far as I could see. Equally important, he knew enough to keep himself nourished. Most of the deterioration of the nervous system produced by taking alcohol over long periods of time is due to the fact that certain vital nutritional elements are oxidized or burned by the alcohol. This man made a practice of eating plenty of good food which made up for the losses. He was healthy and well when I knew him, but then something happened.

During the early years of World War II, for some reason, there was an interval of time, only a few weeks actually, when opium and opium derivatives were in very short supply in Canada. His supply of laudanum ran out and in spite of every effort to obtain the drug, we were unable to get it at once. In about twelve hours he developed uncontrollable nausea and vomiting and soon became dehydrated. Morphine did not seem to have the same effect—perhaps he was sensitive to it. Fluids given into the veins did not help. He died within twenty-four hours. In his own peculiar way, he was a war casualty.

One day in April, about eighteen months after I had come to Canso, I thought I must have a vacation, and decided to take three days off and go and visit my friend Jack Reardin, a dentist, in Prince Edward Island. I had never been there before so I got out a road map and studied the route to Pictou, which is the place from which a ferry goes to the Island. The distance as shown on the map was a hundred and twenty-five miles. The so-called highway was marked by a broad red line and the route was roughly in the shape of the letter L. But on the map there was also a network of fine blue lines which indicated secondary roads. As I looked at them I thought of the proposition in geometry; namely—any two sides of a triangle are longer than the third side. So I thought, instead of taking the red marked route shaped like an L, why not go along the hypotenuse of the triangle by taking the roads marked by the little blue lines. This seemed like good reasoning at the moment, but I was to find that there was something wrong. In this case the hypotenuse turned out to be longer than the other two sides of the triangle. I remember now that even as a boy in school I was suspicious of that particular proposition of Euclid. But at the moment I believed in geometry and I decided on the short cut. Besides the saving in distance, I thought it would be more interesting to go by a less-travelled route.

It happened that on the night before I was to leave, Cragg, my morphine addict, had made his semiannual visit. When I told him of my proposed excursion he asked to be allowed to come along as far as New Glasgow. We started off quite early in the morning as I wanted to have lots of time to catch the ferry which left at four in the afternoon. I knew the first forty miles of the road very well and did not worry about sign posts or directions up to the limit of the forty miles. I was sure that after that the roads would be plainly marked and it would be a simple matter to find the way.

Cragg was a good talker, with a large fund of interesting and curious knowledge picked up in his travels which made him a welcome passenger. He loved to talk, especially about unusual and sometimes bizarre subjects.

"What do you know about Phobos and Deimos?" he asked after he had been silent for three or four minutes.

"Nothing much," I answered, modestly, "except that they are two moons, satellites of Mars, and they must be small because Mars is only a small planet." I was secretly proud to remember so much of my astronomy.

"Well," he said, "Phobos is five thousand, eight hundred miles from the center of Mars and it revolves in a period of seven hours and a half, and Deimos is fourteen thousand miles from the center and revolves in a period of thirty hours."

"Think of that!" I said, thinking only of what a curious character my companion was.

"Yes," he went on. "Swift described them in *Gulliver's Travels*. He described their size roughly, the periods of their revolution and so on. But," Cragg went on, *"Gulliver's Travels* was published in the year, 1726."

"Yes," I said, not seeing the connection.

"Well, the two satellites of Mars were discovered by Hall about one hundred and fifty years later and the first telescope that was invented or built that could possibly have shown them was built about one hundred years after the book was printed."

I began to be interested.

"How did Gulliver know?" he demanded. "Could it be a mere guess? Especially when he foretold that the period of Phobos was so short that it must rise in the west and set in the east, a thing which is unique in the astronomy we know? Here is one sure proven example of somebody knowing something that he could not possibly have known by any natural means. Now," he went on, "I have a theory, and you may think it's crazy, but here is my idea."

He launched into a long and complicated discussion which I cannot duplicate but the gist of it was that Gulliver must have been in telepathic communication with beings in Mars. (I checked later with the *Encyclopedia Americana*, which Cragg gave as a reference, and found that his facts were correct although his theory of the explanation was slightly open to doubt.) But at the time, after an hour or more I realized that I had been driving along mechanically and forgetting to look for route signs. Finally, I knew I was lost. Somewhere along the road, while spellbound by Phobos and Deimos, I must have taken a wrong turn.

Writers of a couple of generations ago used to love to employ a certain story situation that ran like this. A young man starts out, on horseback or on foot, to seek his fortune. He travels along a lonely road watching all the while for possible bandits or highwaymen. He comes to a fork in the road where there is no sign post. He does not know whether to take the right or the left branch. He makes the decision by tossing a coin. The coin tells him to go to the right. From there on he runs into a series of adventures in which he encounters highwaymen, beautiful young girls who have wicked uncles who seek to deprive them of their inheritances, and so on. After a long time the hero lands happily in the arms of the beautiful young heiress and stays there. Now, the author used to like to reflect, what would have happened to the hero if he had taken the road to the left? What other adventures would he have encountered, what other beautiful young ladies in distress would he have rescued?

In real life this happens all the time. Anyone who looks back on his career can pick out more than one point in his journey through life where he was faced with a decision between two separate courses of action. He took the one and rejected the other. What would have been his lot if he had taken the one which he rejected? We never know.

Sometimes I find it amusing, however useless, to speculate on the difference it would have made in my life if I had been alertly watching for the right turn, instead of woolgathering with Cragg and his two moons.

For hours we drove along trails so narrow that the scrub bushes scratched against the sides of the car continuously, and so full of rocks and holes that most of the time we were in low gear and going about five miles an hour. Twice we had to get out of the car and find earth and stones to fill in a deep rut so that the undergear of the car would clear an outcropping rock. At four o'clock in the afternoon when the ferry would be leaving Pictou, we were still in this wilderness. At seven o'clock in the evening we emerged onto a good two-lane gravel highway and found we were eighty miles from Pictou. I had to give up the idea, then, of going to see my friend Jack, because I could not make it in my three-day time limit.

I wondered what to do as an alternative. I had two old classmates practicing in the city of Sydney, about a hundred miles away. Sydney was a steel town and a bustling, lively place. It would be a change from Canso. After debating the matter for the space of time that it takes to smoke two cigarettes, I decided to go there. I let Cragg off at the next town, which was Mulgrave, and three hours later I was in Sydney.

Alix Cohen had been a classmate of mine at medical school who had started to practice in Sydney at the same time as I began work in Canso. I was impressed when I walked into his office. The place was well equipped and there was a general air of prosperity about it. A bright, intelligent-looking girl in a nursing uniform met me in the waiting room. Alix was obviously a success.

We talked for a while, chiefly about cases. Any time two doctors get together, the commonest words used are "I had a case one time," and this exchange of experiences and ideas is the best kind of informal education. The doctor who is a lone wolf and shuns the company of his fellow doctors is at a great disadvantage and is likely not to be a good doctor, although there are some exceptions.

Alix told me something of his career since he had started to practice. He was definitely a success, as a doctor and as a businessman. He was married and was building a new home. He talked of dollars in the same way I talked about pennies. I knew he deserved it. He had been a good, almost-brilliant, student at college. He practiced a good brand of medicine, he was conscientious, and for every dollar he got he gave good and ample service.

When I told him about my situation, he said, "Look, boy, I know the very thing for you. Bill Munster is taking a year off to go to England. He's in New Waterford and he tells me he hasn't found a man yet to take his place while he is away. Why don't you go to see him?"

I was not only interested, I was excited. New Waterford, ten miles from Sydney, was a busy mining town with a big and growing population. If I could get in there, especially stepping in to a ready-made practice, I would have no more financial worries and could soon get my bills paid.

I went to New Waterford that afternoon. As I drove into the town and saw the grimy close-packed company houses, the cinder-paved streets, and the towering smoke-stacks pouring out black smoke into the sky, I had a warm feeling, it was so much like my home town of Inverness. The sulphur and soot in the air smelled better than clover to one who has been brought up with it. The miners in the street looked like old friends. They were just the same as the ones I had known in my boyhood except that they did not appear on the street black—the company provided wash houses—and they did not carry lamps. Miners are, paradoxically, the cleanest people in the world. They take more baths than a movie actress. They are good-hearted people, having a slight contempt for those who work on the surface of the earth just as a sailor looks down on his brothers who are tied to the land. They think little of money as long as the miners are working, and are generous to a fault; they are rough and pretend to be tough, for that is part of the tradition of their brother-hood, but it is only pretense. Actually they are gentle and easygoing. They should not be judged by some of their union leaders, who are a class apart—smart men in a smart profession.

Munster had a very big practice in New Waterford; one of the biggest in fact. He wanted someone right away as he was to leave for England within a week. After half an hour's conversation we made a compact. Under an agreement made a long time ago between the company and the miners, the sum of forty cents was deducted from each miner's pay envelope every week. This amount was turned over to the doctor of the workers' choice. If a man wanted to change doctors he simply signed a card bearing the new doctor's name and turned it in to the pay office. If a doctor had a hundred men on his list he received forty dollars a week. If, as was more usual, he had four or five hundred men on his list he received a hundred and sixty to two hundred dollars a week. In return for this the medical man provided the miner and his family with every type of medical service, plus medicine. Munster did not tell me exactly how many men were paying him under this system, but I know it was a large number. Munster would continue to receive his cheques directly from the company's office and would pay me a monthly salary for doing the work. The salary was distinctly less than the wage of most coal miners who would be my patients, but in those days many of the doctors in Canada were in pretty much the same straits as I was and the law of supply and demand operated effectively to keep salaries down. Besides, I was to receive free room and board. So, although I would earn about five dollars for Munster in England for every dollar I would keep for myself, I was very glad to get the position. At least I would be immeasurably better off financially than I had been before.

Another thing that helped me to make this decision was

the fact that New Waterford was the home of Sally Mac-Neil, whom I had met during my internship years.

During my brief stay in New Waterford and while I was making arrangements with Munster, I had taken no thought of the many strings which held me to Canso and which would have to be broken so abruptly. Back in the place in which I had labored for almost two years I made public the news that I was leaving. I was totally unprepared for the reaction of my patients and I admit I was even surprised at my own emotion.

Inevitably a doctor must have some patients who become attached to him. Sir William Osler once said that it is the privilege of a doctor to save life sometimes, to relieve pain often and to comfort always. Old people particularly turn to their physicians for comfort. They are aware that the sands of time are running low. They may not fear death, but in their loneliness they seek—figuratively speaking—to hold the hand of someone. Some old women openly shed tears in my office; men concealed their emotions more successfully. With young, healthy people of course, it was different. Life was strong in them and they needed less support. A few leaders in the community came to me and coaxed me to stay. There was even talk of a public subscription when I told them I was obliged to leave for financial reasons.

I could not help being moved, and my sensations amounted almost to guilt. Moreover, there was a sense of loss at leaving certain individuals. I felt like a deserter in leaving Jimmy Greenmark, dying of heart disease; I had spent so many hours at his bedside. The fact that there was a good doctor in Guysboro, thirty-five miles away, did little to alleviate my pangs of conscience. So also in the case of eight-year-old Theresa, dying of leukemia.

On the other hand, I could not forget that I was working

toward the achievement of high ambition. I was going to be a brain surgeon, come what might. Whether or not the way lead through New Waterford, it was plain that Canso was a sidetrack.

There were some practical arrangements to be made. I went to my banker. He was not unduly concerned—his bank was a national institution and my account would simply be transferred from his branch to another. To tell the truth, I believe he was a little bit relieved at getting rid of a worrisome client. Fortunately I did not owe very much at the local stores and these debts I was able to liquidate. The great bulk of my obligations lay in the cities of Montreal and Toronto, from where I had bought my drugs and supplies. To the firms in these cities I wrote letters telling of my change of address and assuring them that within a short time they would be paid. I am sure that tears of joy were shed in these faraway offices when they received my letters. There probably was a holiday on St. Catherine Street.

The day of departure came. I said my goodbyes to Mrs. Gary and Mora at six o'clock in the morning. The sun was still low on the horizon as I stepped into my car and its rays brought into relief the tiny boats setting out for the day's fishing. The air was filled with the quick putt-putt of gasoline engines and the sound of rowlocks as men bent to their oars. I drove out of town slowly and with some sadness in my heart.

Chapter Seven

PRACTICE in New Waterford was quite different from practice in Canso. Here there was a denser population and, which made all the difference, a hospital. Every phase of my work was altered, but the change was most pronounced in the field of obstetrics. No longer did I have to go through the long hours of waiting—sometimes in not very comfortable surroundings—in order to be present for a task that might take only five or ten minutes. In a good hospital with a highly trained staff of nurses who know exactly when to call a doctor, there is little occasion for waiting. When I had my first few cases in hospital I thought back upon the couple of hundred of births which I had attended at homes in Canso. I remembered the long hours of dreary waiting during which I was made aware of every single labor pain in greater or less degree—depending upon the self-control of the patient— the importunities of distraught husbands and mothers to "please do something" and the doleful prayers often chanted aloud by female relatives.

In the matter of accurate diagnosis many aids were available which previously had been denied me. The laboratory and the X-ray simplified things very much. Not so often now did I have to go home after seeing a patient and spend sleepless hours racking my brains and wondering whether or not my decision had been correct.

Finally, and perhaps most important, I now had an opportunity of doing surgery of which a great deal came my way. Experience and facility in general surgery are pre-requisites to training for brain surgery. I had as much of this kind of work as anyone could want.

Except for the most highly specialized types, the operations were of every conceivable variety. The most common ones of course were those for appendicitis. In those days there were no antibiotics, so that a ruptured appendix was a much more serious affair than it is now. Operations for hernia were frequent because so many of my patients were men who did hard physical work in the mines. In the summer months tonsils were "in season." They were taken out in bucketsful. When doing a tonsillectomy we usually made a practice of extracting any decayed teeth as part of the procedure. I pulled many thousands. We also did hysterectomies (removal of the womb), nephrectomies (removal of a kidney) and cholecystectomies (removal of the gall bladder), though these were less common. Limb amputations came fairly often because of industrial accidents.

I loved surgery. No matter how many times a doctor performs a particular operation it never becomes a routine, it is never boring. For a short space of time he is an arbiter of life and death. His brain, eye and hand work magic. He is working on something sacred—every good surgeon holds the human body as sacred, in the sense of something to be treated with the greatest respect—and he is acutely aware of it. Writers and moving picture people have made everyone familiar with operating room procedure. They have pictured the gleaming white tiles of the operating room, the bright lights, the white-gowned doctors and nurses. They have described the shiny steel instruments, the quick clean line of incision, the first appearance of red blood, the sponges, the hemostats quickly applied, the sutures quickly tied. They have shown the intent face of the surgeon and the alertness of the quick-moving nurses, but they have failed to tell what goes on in the minds of these people. The surgeon knows that no two operations are exactly alike. The mechanism on which he is working is never exactly the same in two different cases. The large artery or other vital structure is never exactly in the same place as it was in any of his previous cases. The diseased organ may be more difficult or less difficult to approach, the blood vessels may be more difficult to separate and tie, the important nerve more inaccessible. At times during some operations he can work in leisure and think out his next move carefully. Then of a sudden he may find himself racing against time, against minutes, even seconds. Up until the crux of the operation he is in suspense.

There is a good feeling about operating apart from the sense of doing useful work and the feeling of accomplishment. For the space of half an hour, or an hour or two hours, as the case may be, you are in a state of complete detachment from the outside world. Your mind is concentrated so entirely and completely on what you are doing, that nothing can intrude. All other worries, distractions, responsibilities disappear. When you peel off your gloves and leave the operating room it is like coming back from a visit to another world. It is a unique experience and not easy to describe.

Of patients requiring surgical treatment there were more women than men. That is true in almost any hospital. Women may perhaps be said to be more complicated machines. At least they seem to have more troubles that can be treated with a knife. The structures and organs which make up the complex mechanism of reproduction are all subject to diseases which may easily be cured by surgery. The pear-shaped womb may become the seat of a fibroma—a non-malignant and common tumor. The Fallopian tubes which leave the womb and reach with delicate tendrils towards the ovaries may become infected. The ovaries themselves are prone to develop cysts—pockets of fluid material which may become distended to enormous proportions. I remember taking a twenty-two pound tumor out of a woman who weighed only one hundred and six pounds.

Moreover, women are more willing subjects. They are not so apt to shy away at the first mention of an operation, as are men. A few of them, indeed, are all too willing to be operated upon. One woman came to me and stated point-blank that she wanted her womb taken out.

"But why, what is the trouble?" I asked.

"Nothing," she replied. "I just want my womb taken out."

"But," I said, "if there is nothing wrong with you, I can't do an operation like that. Why you—"

She interrupted: "Listen, you took Mrs. X's womb out, didn't you?"

"Well," I explained, "Mrs. X was a sick woman."

"Never mind that," she said. "My husband pays you forty cents a week just as well as her husband does, and if you don't want to do it, he'll turn over his card to someone that will."

Needless to say I did not take her womb out. Her husband did turn in a card for another doctor, but I think, at least I hope, that the lady still has her womb.

The desire to be operated upon when no operation is required is not confined to areas with prepaid medical schemes. Every physician and every surgeon can cite dozens of cases in which people continually and persistently harass him for an operation. These people do not care what is done to them just so long as they have an operation, preferably an abdominal one. A psychiatrist would make something morbid out of this and he might often be right. But I think that in many cases it can be explained by the fact that some people have such dull and uneventful lives that they welcome anything with the appearance of the dramatic, even if it means discomfort or even danger to themselves. It is not often that the most mercenary surgeon will take advantage of this state of mind, but, undoubtedly, in cases where there is not absolute certainty in the doctor's mind as to the absence of disease, it tends to warp his judgment and a needless operation may be performed. The way in which such a case is handled depends, of course, upon the doctor concerned. There are no hard and fast rules for him to follow, and doctors are individuals.

Medical men may develop eccentricities. Some of these may have an important bearing on their work, but most are mild, simple behavior habits and totally harmless. For example, there was the old doctor who used to "trademark" his patients.

One evening I was examining a man and found a long

white scar on his abdomen that showed he had had an operation a good many years ago. At the upper end of the scar there was a little Y-shaped notch. As a rule I would have paid no attention except that I remembered having seen, within the past few weeks, two other people who also bore scars with a similar little notch at the upper end. It occurred to me that this might be more than coincidence, so I asked the patient who had operated on him.

"Oh," he said, "that was old Dr. Ethridge. He's dead a long time now. He was a great old doctor, probably the best surgeon they ever had in this province. Why, they say that when he used to go down to Baltimore on a visit, the big shots there would ask him to operate on some of their hard cases, he was that good."

I heard a great deal about Dr. Ethridge who apparently had died about ten years before. I checked with the other doctors and they told me that they too were familiar with the Y-shaped notches on Dr. Ethridge's incisional scars. It was his fancy to "trademark" patients in this way, just as a jeweler scratches a secret mark or number on the inside of a watch he has repaired. He apparently only did it on abdominal scars, which in those days were never visible to the public eye. It was of course a harmless quirk.

I have often wondered what makes some doctors so outstandingly successful and popular with the public. In a few cases it is, of course, due to extraordinary ability which is so obvious that it becomes recognized by the profession and public alike regardless of what the individual's other qualifications may be. But in every locality large or small you will find some doctor who, though of no special ability, becomes locally famous and whose name is remembered long after he dies.

I knew one doctor who went through medical school as a very average student and who closed all his books the

day after he graduated and never opened them again.
Neither did he ever take a post-graduate course or attend
a medical meeting. He even shut himself off from what is
the most common and profitable form of post-graduate
education of any doctor—the informal and continual discussion of interesting cases with other doctors in the community. Yet he became an unusually successful man,
whose name has long outlived him. I think the secret of
his success may be that he developed an extraordinary
amount of self-confidence by shutting himself off from the
only men who could ever criticize him, his fellow doctors.
His diagnoses were always correct because he never learned
that they were incorrect. If his patients died he could always explain the death as being due to a cause which made
the outcome inevitable. That is, he could explain it to
himself. He was careful not to try to explain it to anyone
else. Did he ever have any secret doubts? I am inclined
to think not. Perhaps he did at the beginning, but I think
that in time he had absolutely none. Needless to say he
did a good deal of harm, but he did a great deal of good
too, because he was a tireless worker and most of his work
was well done.

There was another doctor who became famous because
he loved liquor so much. At least two weeks out of every
month would be spent on benders. He would disappear
from his office and be unavailable to the public—dead
drunk for one or two weeks at a time. Everyone knew it.
They used to pick him literally out of the gutter, unconscious, and take him home. I don't know why it is, but a
professional man who is addicted to alcohol gets a reputation for having a brilliant mind. "He'd be the most
brilliant doctor [or lawyer] in the whole country if only
he'd stay sober" is a sentence I'm sure everyone has heard.

Some doctors have a naturally dramatic, almost theatrical, way of doing things. Their appearance is imposing, their movements deliberate. The simple act of taking a thermometer from a patient's mouth and reading it can be done with the air of Madame Curie looking at the first sample of radium. Such a man will not say, "I'm afraid the boy's got a touch of pneumonia. We'll have to give him some penicillin." No, he will carefully put away his instruments, stand up, pause, and utter the single word "pneumonia" in a deep voice charged with significance. The anxious parents, their eyes fixed on him, repeat "pneumonia, pneumonia?" His answer is, "Quick, the telephone." Or if he happens to be a surgeon and has just finished an operation, let us say a tonsillectomy or an appendectomy, he will appear in the waiting room, where the anxious parents or relatives are gathered, his operating room gown still on and effectively splattered with just the right amount of blood. In a grave and deliberate voice he says, only, "The child will live." The relatives break out in smiles of joy and relief. "What a wonderful man! What an incomparable doctor!" they think. He turns and walks away. This manner to some men is not deliberate affectation. They take to it naturally, without any conscious desire of impressing the public. But there are some unfortunately who play to the grandstand, and do it deliberately, using all kinds of little tricks. These men may carry on a long time, but generally people see through them after a while.

These odd types do not of course represent the typical successful doctor. Ninety-five percent of the men who become well and favorably known and stand out among their fellow practitioners before the public, accomplish this simply by being hard and conscientious workers, whose great determination and singleness of purpose—how often have I heard my old college professors extol these virtues

—carry them in a line straight and true as an arrow towards their goal in life. Others move forward in a zigzag fashion, deflected this way and that by various forces from without. I was one of the latter.

The star of my ambition shone as brightly as ever. While severing the femoral nerve in the course of doing a leg amputation I knew I *should* be at work reaching for the sensory root of the Fifth Cranial Nerve hidden under the temporal lobe of the brain. Every time I removed a gall bladder I wished myself at work on a neuroglioma of the cerebellum.

But when all my thought and energy should have been concentrated on securing the nine thousand eight hundred dollars I needed so badly, a comet in the form of the clear-eyed Sally came into proximity. The gravitational pull was enormous. Nevertheless, for a time I steered clear of her sphere of influence.

I should like to say that this was due to my great strength of character, but I must admit that I received minor aid from one or two circumstances. First of all I was so broke that the purchase of a new shirt was a financial transaction to be considered as carefully as the buying of another steel mill by Henry Ford. Secondly, and more important, the comet showed no indication whatever of being aware of my presence. A germ on a glass slide under the microscope had more chance of attracting her attention, I thought ruefully. This was the situation when a local character bearing the unlikely nickname of Bad Chris stepped into the picture. He was to play the role of Cupid —a part that outwardly seemed as well suited to him as the part of Rebecca of Sunnybrook Farm to Joe Louis.

The town of New Waterford did not have exactly what would be called in a big city, an "underworld," but like most towns of its size it had a group of characters who spent much of their time in less-than-lawful activities. They did not like work and they had a strong flair for drinking and fighting. Fist fights on the main street, in the alleys, and back of stores were almost a daily occurrence. On pay-day, which was Saturday, there might be two or three of these fights going on in different parts of one street at the same time. The crowds of cheerful onlookers would be kept busy running up and down from one fight to the other.

One night just as I was nearly through with my office work and was wearily looking forward to crawling into bed, a man appeared in the doorway of my consulting room who looked like William Bendix, Victor McLaglen, Maxie Rosenbloom and Boris Karloff rolled into one. He leaned against the doorjamb for a minute looking at me without saying a word.

"Well, come in," I said, "what can I do for you?" He mumbled something but did not move except to fumble at the door with both hands. He was extremely drunk and I saw that he could barely stand up.

I spoke to him again with no more satisfaction. My patience was at an end, and realizing he was so drunk that he could hardly move, I told him to get out and I am afraid I did not use very gentle language. He gave me a look and then without trying to say another word he turned and half staggered, half fell out of my office. The next day I told my colleague and friend, Angus MacMillan, about the episode.

"Good God," he said, "you certainly pick on the wrong kind of people to order out of your office. That was Bad Chris. He'll come back when he gets to be only half drunk and he'll pound the daylights out of you."

I knew Angus meant what he said, so it was with some apprehension that I opened up the office the following evening. Sure enough, Bad Chris arrived and sat down in the waiting room in a state halfway between drunk and sober and looking very ugly and mean. There were a lot of patients waiting and he sat unmoving in a corner. It was obviously his intention to wait until I was through with everyone else and then see me alone. I was a little bit distracted with the other patients that night, I'm afraid. I was all for keeping them as long as possible but it seemed that the crowd in the waiting room dwindled with surprising speed and soon there was no one left except Bad Chris. He walked into my office with great deliberation. I braced myself, determined to sell my life as dearly as possible when suddenly I had an inspiration.

"Look, Bad Chris," I said, "am I glad to see you! You came in at exactly the right time. I just got a call to go down to Lennoxville." (This was true.) "There's an awfully tough crowd down there and I was wondering if I should get a couple of policemen to come with me for a bodyguard. How about you coming with me instead? That is," I added, "if you have the time."

I could see a change come over the knobby features. He did not say anything for almost a full minute. Then he said, "Sure, Doc, I got time. Let's go."

His voice was gruff and rasping but I knew he was pleased and proud. His grudge had disappeared.

From that day on, Bad Chris became one of my greatest boosters, as well as my friend. He hung around the office, polished my car for me—the only lawful work he ever did, I believe—and accompanied me on long and lonely calls. He talked a good deal. During our conversations he held forth on the state of the Union (I mean the local branch of the United Mine Workers of America), and on philosophy and metaphysics of a very high order. He had no education but I am sure that certain doctors of philosophy

I know could have learned much from him. One of his favorite propositions was: "To hell with tomorrow. It don't belong to us. Live right now, is what I always say." He had something there. Many great philosophers have spent a lifetime learning as much.

One day he told me that a graduate nurse named Miss MacNeil had, as he expressed it, "given him hell" for having insulted a student nurse. He confided in me that he had debated with himself between drowning this Miss MacNeil, choking her or throwing her down a pit shaft but that he had ended up by apologizing instead. That such an innocent-looking creature as my comet could have so twisted the ear of this giant greatly impressed me. Obviously, with such a girl by my side—if I could persuade her—I would be able to move steadily towards my goal instead of continually being deflected from it.

It is so easy to invent arguments in favor of what one wants to do! The old maxim that "he travels fastest who travels alone" suddenly struck me as silly. I looked for counter-maxims and I found quantities.

Once properly started it didn't take long to convince myself that the quickest way to reach the pinnacle of success was to take Sally along with me. Now came the problem of convincing Sally. How could I reconcile the fact that I had managed to slide so deeply into debt in my two years of practice with the proposition that some day I was going to be the greatest brain surgeon in the whole world? I invented all kinds of theories and spent hours figuring out the exact wording for my arguments.

Later I was to learn that all my carefully prepared statements might as well have had to do with the political problems of the Balkan states or the question of the origin of species. In other words, she paid no attention to them. Probably she had not even listened while I was talking so earnestly. I think the eventual outcome of my campaign can be credited to some mischievous sprite who liked to snarl up the lives of humans and had at the moment singled out Sally for his victim.

We were married on January twenty-sixth. It sounds simple saying it that way. I suppose a man like Eisenhower, with his keen cold brain and genius for organization, could reduce the terrific confusion that reigns for three weeks before a wedding to some kind of order and make things go in a precise way. Sally had to work up until three days before the wedding because they could not at once get a replacement for her at the hospital, and I had to work right up until it was time to go to the church. During the last weeks there were parties, presentations, showers, etc. Sally had to shop for dresses, cake, and so on, in between hours of duty. There were arrangements of all kinds to be made, consultations, countless telephone calls that made the wires grow hot and threatened to break down the entire communications system of the country.

I remember a few things about the wedding. It took place at four o'clock in the morning because the only train out of town left at seven. There was new snow on the ground and the night was clear and very cold—it is very much night at four A.M. in January, in Nova Scotia. The church looked like a painting on a Christmas card.

I remember a wedding breakfast at which someone gave a long speech praising Sally, the MacNeil family, the MacNeil clan, the isle of Barra—the home of the MacNeils in the Hebrides—the Scottish race, and the whole of Scotland. I was interested only in Sally and yet here I was involved with the whole of Scotland. The speaker very generously admitted that it was possible from time to time for an individual of another race to rise above the handicap of not being Scotch, but he implied that it happened only very rarely. I began to feel like a worm, like an intruder who should never have dared look at Sally, let alone marry her. I remember being grateful to Sally's mother for a sympathetic look. She was born with the name Farrell and the Irish part of her may have rebelled. I think the speaker must have guessed how I was feeling because in the end he paid me a terrific compliment. He said that he had been in my brother George's store one time and that George had seemed to him to be "not a bad sort."

I remember a few other things. I remember some people admiring the wedding gifts and saying, "Oh!" when they saw my gift to the bride. It was a cheque for five hundred dollars, made out to Sally and signed by me. I think now that some of them must have guessed at the time that it was for show purposes only and not intended to be cashed. "Oh!" can have quite a few meanings.

I remember a poor old man at the railway station—he was very old and very poor—who stood shivering in the morning cold. He was a man I had treated a few times. In his mittened hands he held a parcel and just as we were getting on the train he pushed it at me. When I opened it later, it turned out to be a bottle of brandy. What he sacrificed to buy this bottle of brandy I don't know, but I still choke up a little when I think of it.

I remember that on the train we met an old acquaintance of mine who relieved the monotony of the first few hours of our honeymoon by talking to us about the co-operative movement and the need for introducing a type of socialism that would really serve the interests of the people.

Finally I remember the plane which we boarded at New Glasgow and which took us to Charlottetown, Prince

Edward Island. It was an old plane that sat on skis instead of wheels. Its wings were made of fabric that needed patching in places and one of its engines looked as though it were ready to fall out—in fact I think it would have fallen out if I hadn't kept watching it all the time. But it was a lovely ship and it carried us safely through the clouds.

When we got back from our honeymoon, we moved into four rooms which an elderly couple on Scotchtown Road had converted into a self-contained flat for us, for a rental that amounted to about one third of my salary. A friendly and very trusting merchant had supplied it with furniture on the installment plan so that we had a bedroom, a sitting room, a dining room and a kitchen. They were all nice new things and we were proud of them. The sitting room had a studio couch and two chairs.

I have read a great many articles on the general subject of Adjustment to Marriage, but all of them have been very inferior—they have left out the most important things. Probably because the authors didn't dare mention them. For example, I remember my wonder when I found out that Sally required food three times a day. In my childhood days I had somehow come to believe that really nice girls did not eat. When I say "nice girls" I mean the kind you dream about, not the uninteresting ones like sisters and cousins and girls who live next door. A girl like Sally, I thought, should live on ocean air and sunlight. They might eat an occasional pickle or a little ice cream—just to show their democratic spirit—but not real food like steak and potatoes, roast beef and vegetables.

Again I found that Sally had many strange, unusual ideas. She considered it important, for instance, to have curtains and drapes on windows. Not only that but she thought they should be of certain colors. Now I had always taken curtains for granted. They were things that were just there—not things that had to be measured and bought and hung up in a certain way. Nor had I realized that things had to be cleaned, ordinary things like stoves and furniture and sinks, and that floors had to be waxed and polished. I began to realize that married life was a pretty complicated business after all.

In spite of all these disillusionments, however, we gradually got used to the new ways and began to settle down to normal living. I say "began" because we were hardly under way when we realized that a stranger was with us. His name was Worry.

It was really all Sally's fault. She should not have concealed from me the fact that she was almost as poor at mathematics as I was. I had taken it for granted that a girl like her would know all about X squared plus XY plus Y squared being equal to something or other and therefore be able to figure out telephone and light bills. If she had only known that Y is equal to F (x) she might have been able to deal with the grocery man on equal terms. But no, she was as helpless as I. But we tried! We called our salary Q and our expenditures EX and worked at it for hours, but the net result was the same. We always ended up with a minus quantity, in other words, by owing somebody. I think a law should be passed requiring people who are going to be married not only to have a blood test but to pass an examination in the essentials of the integral and differential calculus.

In the past the lack of money had meant to me simply delay in getting started on my real career. But now lack of money had a different significance. It meant the imminent prospect of lack of food, the prospect of having no coal to put in the stove and the curtailment of various little luxuries like going to a movie every week and smoking cigarettes. Sally tried to make light of those things. She said she had always liked hamburg better than roast beef anyhow, and that it was a good thing to give up smoking. It would make us healthier. Just the same I didn't feel any healthier.

As time went on things became worse instead of better. We talked about it all the time, morning, noon and evening. It was just as well that we ate hamburg and bologna instead of steak or lamb chops. We couldn't have noticed the flavor anyway, what with our talk about bills and overdrafts and the possibility of the light company turning off the power.

It was at Sally's suggestion that we instituted "Worrying Sessions" as part of our family routine. We agreed one day that we would refrain from discussing financial troubles of any sort except for a certain period of each evening. At first these sessions were not too grim. Actually the open talking about our affairs was a kind of relief after some of the silent thinking of the day.

When things got very bad we used a special technique. We would read together Cherry-Garrard's *The Worst Journey in the World*. At once we were transported down to the Antarctic with Scott on his last expedition. There we were in a tent, a blizzard howling around us, the temperature fifty degrees below zero, nothing to eat but a little dog-meat and the gasoline in our primus stove running low—separated from home and civilization by hundreds of miles of dead barren ice and snow. From our tent down in the Antarctic we could see things like banks and debts and so on in their true perspective. If any reader has worries I recommend that he get a copy of Cherry-Garrard's book if he can find one. Our copy is dog-eared and worn.

Chapter Eight

Bill MUNSTER came back from England a few months earlier than he had planned. His return posed a problem for us. We were now free to go into practice for ourselves in New Waterford. That had been part of the agreement between him and me. If we did this we would make very much more money—some of our doctor friends in the area had very good incomes. We hoped to do as well, and began to lay our plans. And it was now that we ran into an unforeseen complication.

There was a peculiar regulation regarding doctors in the original agreement between the coal company and the miners. Before the company would put a doctor's name on their list and check off the miners' forty cents for him, he must first have one quarter of the total number of miners in one particular colliery agree to have him for their personal physician. The smallest colliery in the area was Colliery Number Thirty-Two. As this mine employed eight hundred and twenty men, that meant that at least two hundred and five men must turn in to the office a signed card agreeing to have their weekly payroll deduction turned over to me.

It was not sufficient to have two hundred and five men in town who were willing to do this; they must all be working at this particular colliery. Now the direct soliciting of patients is expressly forbidden by all rules of medical ethics so I could not directly ask any miner to sign a card for me. I could not use any publicity or make any kind of appeal whatever. It seemed that the only thing to do was *hope* that two hundred and five men all working in Number Thirty-Two would guess that I wanted to get on the payroll, would come looking for me and ask me for a card and sign it!

I turned to the other doctors for advice and they gave me not only advice but some direct help. Most of them agreed to "lend" me patients, that is, ask some of their miner patients to sign over to me temporarily until I got on the payroll. This was not too easy to do because most of the miners, being young healthy men, very seldom came near the doctor—it was their wives and families who kept him busy. Again, only men working in Number Thirty-Two were eligible. Nevertheless we got some sixty names in this way. Two of my friends helped me particularly— Duncan Campbell, a successful and highly regarded physician in New Waterford—and Angus MacMillan.

With only sixty names I was stalled. Sally and I spent hours every night talking over the situation. There was no more income, now that Munster was back. On the other hand there was rent to pay, grocery, light, fuel and telephone bills. On top of that I had to maintain an office and I still made calls, though there was no pay, because it was a cardinal rule—made by the doctors themselves—that if a miner ever needed a doctor and could not find his own at once, he could call any other man in town and that man would have to respond.

Every night, Sally and I sat and talked. The bills owing got bigger. Our total debt was now well over the five thousand mark—actually nearer six than five. Letters from the creditors to whom we owed that money were becoming more and more disagreeable. We dreaded getting the mail every day and even sometimes found excuses for not opening it. Years after I found an unopened letter among some old papers, containing a cheque for ten dollars!

One night we were sitting on our unpaid-for studio couch engaged in our favorite topic of conversation, when there was a knock at the door. It was a loud strong knock and yet in a way there was something hesitant about it. There is a difference in knocks—pages could be written on the subject—and this one sounded interesting. Later I was to compare it with the knock of an angel, until Sally pointed out that the comparison was irreverent. I opened the door and before me stood Bad Chris. Although there was a strong smell of rum about him I was glad to note that he was not very drunk—at least not more so than usual. He walked pretty steadily as he made his way into our living room and sat down, cap in hand. I was a little surprised to see him. It was seldom that he visited me in the evenings.

"I'm glad to see you, Bad Chris," I said. "How's everything going with you?"

"Not too bad, Doc," he said. Silence followed.

I said, "How are the children?"

"Fine."

"And the Mrs.?"

"Fine." More silence. It was not easy to make conversation with Bad Chris.

"I hear you're wanting to get on the payroll, Doc," he said finally. "Is that right?"

"It certainly is," I replied, looking at my wife.

"I can get you on," he said, and then he added—"easy."

"Well," I said, "I certainly am anxious to get on, but I don't see—"

"I got a gang, Doc. I'll get the boys to go out and canvass for you. Get it all done in no time."

"I haven't got any money to pay the boys, Bad Chris. I wouldn't want them to lose any working hours on my account." The reference to working hours was hypocrisy on my part. I knew that few of his gang ever worked.

He looked at me with a superior smile.

"Don't worry about pay, Doc. The boys'll be happy if you just slip them the odd drink once in a while when they come in with the cards. We'll get the ball rolling tomorrow morning. Goodbye, Doc."

He got up and started for the door. At the threshold he paused.

"Say, Doc, you don't happen to have a drink on you?" he asked.

My spirits fell back to their normal level, which was in my boots. This was only another ruse for cadging a drink. The half pint of Scotch which I had hidden under the studio couch and which we had been saving for the night —to help us think—was about to take wings. I hesitated only a moment.

"Sure thing, Bad Chris, sorry I didn't think of offering you one before. Wait a minute." I fetched the bottle and was going to get a glass, when he stopped me.

"Never mind the glass, Doc, this'll do." He took the bottle from my hand, threw his head back and poured the half pint of neat spirits down without stopping for a single breath. He handed back the empty bottle without saying a word, turned and marched out of the door. When he had gone I looked at Sally who had been watching the performance. She began to cry silently.

We sat down and quickly got ourselves lost in the Antarctic. Sally dried her tears—lest they get frozen—but I noticed that her face looked a little pinched.

The next morning at about ten o'clock there was another knock at the door, and in came a queer-looking, one-eyed, unshaven and uncombed little man whom I recognized as Cadillac Smith—he got the name because he had once served a jail term for stealing a car of that make —whom I had seen in company with Bad Chris on one or two occasions. He passed me five white cards.

"I got five names, Doc," he said proudly, "and I just started an hour ago."

To say that I was amazed would be putting it mildly. Bad Chris had not been deceiving us after all! Suddenly he and Cadillac became elevated in my estimation to the stature of gentlemen of the highest order. I made a mental resolution there and then never to judge a man harshly just because he is considered a drunk and counted by the public as being "no good." That is one resolution I have managed to keep through the years. Time has taught me that there are very few "no good" people in the world.

I told Cadillac in no uncertain language how surprised and pleased I was.

"It's nothing, Doc. I'll have twenty-five before the day is over. Wait and see. And the other boys are hard at it, too." He stood there waiting expectantly while I was trying to think of something to say.

"Look, Cadillac," I said, "this is grand of you. I wish I had a drink to offer you but I haven't a drop in the house, but," I hastened to say when I saw his face fall, "I'll have some a little later. You drop back in a little while, will you, please?"

When he went out I turned to Sally. She was up to her elbows in dough—she had old-fashioned ideas about home-made bread.

"Look," I said, "this is an emergency and it appears that we will have to invest a little money. I'm going down to the liquor store and—"

She stopped me.

"Oh no, you're not," she said, and I was surprised at the note of determination in her voice. "If you want to, I'll serve them cake and tea when they come in. But we are not going to use liquor to bribe people into working for us. I'd rather starve first!"

I looked at her with admiration. She had flour on her nose and in her hair, as well as on her hands and arms, but it looked good on her. Still I did not give in at once.

"Tea and cake for Bad Chris and Cadillac Smith!" I exclaimed. "The trouble with you is that you don't understand men of this type. They'd laugh at us and then —no more cards."

"Laugh or no laugh, it'll do them good. And anyway, there's going to be no doling out of gin."

"But all the big politicians do it," I argued, without much conviction.

"Never you mind the politicians," she said. "That's different and perhaps they have to do it. I don't know. Anyway we are not going to do it."

I argued a little more but my heart was not in it, so I lost. I began to dread the return of Cadillac and his friends. I almost felt as if I were betraying a sacred trust.

I resigned myself to Fate and began to frame words of apology. "You know how it is with women, boys," I fancied myself saying. "They're kind of funny in some ways. But anyway thanks for your good intentions. I'm sorry. I'm awfully sorry, but it can't be helped. Never mind about the cards. I'll manage somehow." I almost worked myself up to tears thinking about it.

Within half an hour Cadillac was back with two more cards. I felt miserable when I saw the eagerness and pride with which he handed them to me. With him was another man called Johnny Forbes. He was a stout, soft-looking man, well-dressed compared to Cadillac, but with a nervous tic which made him screw up the left side of his face regularly every thirty seconds. Johnny had four cards which he gave me with a big smile.

I braced myself for my speech of apology and began mumbling a few words when Sally breezed into the room miraculously free of dough and flour and dressed up as if about to entertain royalty.

"I'm so glad to see you, boys," she said, in her brightest and most cheerful manner. "My husband has been telling me the nicest things about you, how you've been helping us by getting cards and all that. Now you must be tired. Please make yourselves comfortable and in a minute I'm going to bring you each a nice cup of tea and some cake."

I will never forget the expressions of astonishment on the faces of my visitors. Johnny Forbes' jaw dropped and I think that for a minute or two his face stopped twitching. When Sally brought in the tray and began to pass things around they sat awkwardly and said, "Thanks, Ma'am," and answered, "Yes Ma'am" and "No Ma'am," in answer to her questions. I tried to make conversation, but there were long periods of strained silence. They dutifully ate their cake and drank a cup of tea, but they firmly and manfully refused a second helping. With their last mouthful they were on their feet and explaining that they had work to do. Quickly they made off—to spread the word around among their comrades, I was sure. In this estimate it turned out that I had judged correctly, because for the rest of the day we saw no more of them. Sally hopefully kept the teapot in readiness all day but she had no guests.

The next day came and went without any word from our helpers. I didn't blame them. According to their code I had let them down, and therefore was not a good sport. I was strongly tempted to go looking for Bad Chris and, in some back-handed manner, break the law as laid down by Sally. I debated this question for perhaps an hour before I knew that I couldn't do it. And with that I was assailed by a certain bitterness.

Generally speaking, every youth starting the long period of studies which leads to his becoming a doctor, has all of youth's ideas about doing good in the world, being a champion of the oppressed and suffering, and doing work that is at once exciting and spectacular. When he thinks of the actual practice of medicine, he visualizes himself in a community where people need him and look to him to save their lives or ease their pain. He does not think of money. He sneers if he hears an older and wiser doctor talking on the subject of "collections." I am sorry to say that I myself have done some of that sneering. Never in those earlier days had the thought occurred to me that before becoming a rescuer of the sick and helpless I might have to go through anything like this undignified campaign.

That day we had cake for breakfast, cake for lunch and cake for dinner in the evening.

The next day was a little better. Sally found six potatoes in a dark corner of a cupboard when she was cleaning and that evening we had a wonderful dinner of Potatoes and Point. Point is unquestionably one of the most remarkable foods in the world. I am surprised that it is not mentioned in the *Boston Cook Book,* but doubtless it will appear in a future edition. It means boiled potatoes served with nothing else but salt and pepper and imagination. It was invented, I believe, by an old sea cook who, when he found the pork barrel empty during an extra-long voyage, suspended the last tiny scrap of meat by a string from the ceiling of the galley so that each member of the crew could point to it between bites of boiled potato. Whether the story is true or not I do not know. Anyway, the term Potatoes and Point is commonly used in some parts of Cape Breton to designate a very skimpy meal.

At about ten o'clock that evening we were astonished by the sudden reappearance of Bad Chris at our door. He was in a sorry-looking state. His lower lip was bruised and swollen, he had a cut on his cheek and one eye was turning blue. He had a strange story to tell, a story which we could hardly believe at first but which turned out to be true. It appeared that the day after we had seen him, he had encountered a hoodlum by the name of Benny Arkay. This man had told him that he and his gang were soliciting names for a certain Dr. Link who had arrived in town quietly the night before and who also wanted to get on the payroll. Link, I knew, was practicing in the neighboring city of Sydney, but it seems that he was desirous of moving to New Waterford. How he had come into contact with Benny I do not know. Arkay and Bad Chris had been enemies for a long time. My friend confessed that when Cadillac had brought him the news of the cake and tea, he had to employ some persuasion to get his boys to work. But after the encounter with the rival gang they had pitched in with zeal. Drinks or no drinks, they had their pride to consider. All day the rival gangs had gone about soliciting "votes" for their respective "candidates" and now and again they clashed. Just before coming to our apartment Bad Chris had been jumped by two of Arkay's boys. Chris had knocked both of them out cold and they were now, he supposed, being looked after by Dr. Link. He produced from his pocket a box and handed it to me.

"Here you are, Doc," he said, "two hundred and twelve of them. Now you're in."

I thanked Chris with as much enthusiasm as I could muster—I think I made a pretty good show of it, because he seemed to be satisfied—but the victory brought no elation. While I worked at repairing some of the damage to the face of my champion I had some odd thoughts. For a moment I almost wished I had really gone on to be an astronomer.

Ten days later we got our first cheque. It was for eighty-two dollars. We were elated. Eighty-two dollars a week was three hundred and twenty-eight dollars a month and that, we were sure, was only the beginning. The practice would grow and grow and we did not see why we should not be earning about a thousand dollars a month within a year. This was more like it, we thought. That same afternoon we drove down to an automobile sales room to look at a display of new Hudsons. We were not buying, just yet, we told the man, but would be in the market for a new car in a very short time. That night too, I sat down and wrote a lot of reassuring letters to our creditors, all of them beginning with, "You will be glad to learn that—" and ending with the sentence, "You may rest assured that the entire amount will be liquidated in a very short time."

Just as we thought, the practice grew and grew; that is

the phone rang all day long and often during the night, and my office was filled with people of all descriptions. I was very busy. Sally was busy too, making plans for fixing up the apartment as soon as we had all the creditors paid off (What is four or five thousand dollars when you soon will be making a thousand a month?) and in the meantime cooking and baking and doing all the decorating that could be done without money. We were having a wonderful time. The second week our cheque was for eighty-three dollars and twenty cents. "You see," we said to each other, "it is starting to climb already." We did not admit that we were a little disappointed in the size of the increase.

The next week the cheque was down to sixty dollars. I explained to Sally very carefully that this decrease was only temporary. It was due, I said, to the fact that the patients who had been "loaned" to us by the other doctors to help us get on the payroll, had now signed back to them. We were still quite cheerful about it but we did not talk about the new Hudson any more. The next week we got forty-two dollars and eighty cents and the week after, thirty dollars.

It may seem strange that as I did increasingly more work my income continued to drop. The explanation is a simple one when the peculiar local factors are understood. The miners had a strong sense of loyalty and it was a point of honor with them to keep paying their old doctor, even though they might never be able to find him when they needed attention. Moreover, they were well aware of the existing medical code which put every physician at their service although they paid only one. I know an elderly, and very good doctor in one of the colliery towns who has hardly done a stroke of work for the past many years, but who still has a very fine income. Incredible? It is perfectly true.

In the following weeks our income dropped down to twenty-six, to twenty-four and then to twenty dollars. At the same time because of the increased amount of work I was doing, I had contracted new debts for drugs and supplies to the amount of several hundred dollars. There is no doubt that in time this situation would have righted itself, our income would have started to climb and eventually would probably have reached the figures for which we hoped. But our creditors were getting very disagreeable again. We began to receive letters, now, with "Final Warning" printed in red across the top. They no longer hinted but told in unpleasant detail of all the disagreeable things their lawyers would do. I was compelled to admire the skillful wording of these letters and the way in which they could convey the maximum of refined insult in a small paragraph or two. The people who composed these letters were, I could see, very shrewd and had probably spent years in perfecting their art.

In the midst of this slightly disturbing situation we learned that in due time we were to be visited by a "joyous event." Any couple who has ever received notice of a "joyous event" in the midst of an avalanche of letters with "Final Warning" written at the top, will realize what this meant to us.

We tried to think of new ways of saving money. One of our friends had an Austin Seven of the same age as our Ford. We made an even trade, a profitable arrangement on both sides. He got a car which was worth more on the used auto market, and we got a car which gave us a mileage of forty to fifty miles to the gallon.

We spent night after night debating one course of action after another, our ideas becoming more and more fantastic. I remember the day I saw a notice in the *Canadian Medical Journal* stating that the British Imperial Army would accept two doctors from Canada for service with the British troops in India. I came home all excited. I told Sally we were moving to Bombay and we spent the whole of our worrying session that evening reading about India instead of the South Pole, and the next day I astonished the ticket agent at the railway station by asking him what it would cost for two people to go to Bombay, India.

Chapter Nine

ON THE crest of a hill overlooking Halifax harbor—
across the water from the city—there is an unusual building. It is long, shaped roughly like a broad V and looks
rather like an ancient castle. The central portion is four-
stories high, with large stone pillars at the entrance, and
the wings, each of which is about as long as a city block,
are of brick and stone, completely covered with ivy. Surrounding the building is a huge expanse of well-kept lawn,
extending almost to the water's edge, where there are
winding paths with well-trimmed edges, immense shade
trees and numerous flower beds. There is nothing here to
suggest the grim or sinister.

It is possible that if I had said to Sally, when I was trying to persuade her to marry me, "We will live in a tar-

papered shack up in the hills, where the only running water
is in a brook fifty feet away, and eat wild rabbits and oat-
meal," she might still have done it. She is reckless in some
ways. But I know that if I had said, "Come marry me and
we will live happily in a lunatic asylum," she would have
replied, "I'm sorry, dear, and I will always cherish your
memory and love you as a brother, but I think I'll wait
for the King of Sweden or Lord Vanderbilt, or somebody
like that. I can't exactly see myself honeymooning in a
lunatic asylum."

Yet, on a lovely day in early June, we moved into our
new home—a hospital for the violently insane. . . .

Months of worrying and planning in our little apartment in New Waterford, of exploring this possibility and
that, had ended when my friend Dr. MacEachern, superintendent of the Nova Scotia Hospital, had informed me,
in the course of a chance visit, of a temporary vacancy on
the staff. They needed an assistant physician to relieve,
for a period of one year. The salary was one hundred dollars a month plus full maintenance. I put in an application, and as mine was the only one, it was accepted. Ap-
palling as the idea of living in such a place might be for a
bride of five months, Sally took it well. Actually, it was
not a difficult decision for either of us. With a baby coming we needed a roof over our heads, food and security for
a time, at least.

A mental institution was, in the old days, entirely and
solely a prison. Today there has been a slight, but only
slight, advance made in the treatment of diseases of the
mind, so that it is also partly a hospital. It is still, however, more prison than hospital. It has strong doors, bars
and keys. The inmates are of all types and ages, young
and old, men and women, rich and poor, good and bad,

intelligent and stupid—almost all of them here for their own protection or for the protection of others.

Our apartment was on the second floor of the center portion of the building, directly over the administration offices. It had five large rooms and two bathrooms. The furniture was old-fashioned but very good, preserved intact from a generation gone by; it would cost many thousands of dollars today to duplicate it. But the big rooms had plenty of windows, and the walls, the high ceilings and the massive woodwork were painted in bright modern colors. The baths were modern, and there was a kitchenette of the newest design, completely equipped but was used by us only for preparing lunches at odd times or, occasionally, for entertaining friends in privacy. We took our meals in the staff dining room which was just across the hallway from our apartment—a beautiful living arrangement.

No millionaire could have bought better service than we had. There were people to do the chores, the sweeping, dusting and other things; the laundry was called for and brought back without our lifting a finger. Besides the paid employees who took the responsibility for these routine duties, we had dozens of willing helpers for anything else we might need. These were the patients on parole. There was an appreciable number of inmates who were not well enough to return to life in the outside world, but who nevertheless did not need to be kept behind locked doors during the daylight hours. They had the run of the grounds and, within limits, could do pretty well as they pleased. Most of them were anxious to work and did so at one or another of the scores of occupations involved in the upkeep of a large hospital. If they did not want to work they simply walked about the grounds and did whatever took their fancy. Theirs was not an unhappy life.

Dr. MacEachern was a short wiry man, bristling with energy, kind and tolerant but firm, and with a rare sense of humor—a most valuable asset for the work in which he was engaged. Dr. Miriam Houghton, who was in charge of the women's section, I did not come to know as well because I had little to do with her department, but I found that she was a good physician and that her patients loved her. Mr. Lewison, chief in charge of the male attendants, had a very mild gentle manner which never altered even under the greatest provocation. The most violent and difficult of the two or three hundred patients in the men's section would allow themselves to be led by him and would follow his directions.

I used to make rounds with Mr. Lewison every morning—examining the patients who were physically sick (of whom there were very few) and talking to every patient who wanted to talk. Usually they would have some little request, for a sleeping draught, for medicine for little, fancied ailments they could think up, and most often for more tobacco. Mr. Lewison always had one pocket full of cigarettes and another full of little squares of compressed pipe tobacco. Each of the "strong-rooms," in which the most violent and destructive patients were confined, was opened and the patients inspected.

There were three or four patients who had to be force-fed every day. All of those I saw were of the catatonic type of dementia praecox. They would never tolerate any clothes. They would sit absolutely motionless; knees drawn up, head bent, arms folded across the chest, day in and day out for months and in some cases for years. They seemed to be as unconscious of heat or cold as they were of everything else around them. They were fed once a day. Two attendants would stand on either side of the patient, one would force his mouth open by prying it with a small wooden wedge and then it was my duty to quickly push a long rubber tube down into his stomach. When this tube was in place, a specially prepared solution was poured down. This consisted principally of eggs, milk and glucose. At first, it seemed to me senseless, almost cruel, to force these people to stay alive, but I learned from Dr. MacEachern that he had known an occasional patient who had been forced to take nourishment for many years, suddenly to begin eating of his own accord, come out of the long trance, and in time become perfectly well. But even he admitted that such happy cases were rare.

There was a clergyman there, a patient, whom I knew very well—I had known him a long time before he became mentally ill. To avoid embarrassment he was known on the ward simply as Mr. Smith, and was indistinguishable in dress from any other patient. He was an unusually intelligent, perhaps a brilliant, man, extremely well-educated, a student and a scholar in the real sense of the word. He had always been a good, kind and tolerant man before his illness, and apparently well adjusted in every phase of his life, just the opposite of what we commonly call "neurotic." No psychiatrist could ever explain why a man like this should become insane, although I know some would try. I used to take him for walks around the hospital grounds and he often tried to explain to me how it felt to be insane.

"It's like this," he would say. "My mind seems to go around and work so fast and I can't stop it. Let me give you an example. You say to me, 'How are you today, Mr. Smith?' Now, I answer you right away without hesitation. I don't hesitate even a split second, but in that split second, this is what I think: What does he mean by saying, 'How are you today?' Does he want to know how I am mentally or physically or does he really want to know anything at all. That is a mechanical phrase, 'How are you today?' It really does not deserve an answer at all. Wasted words, wasted words, wasted words. Words should not be wasted. Should I answer him or not? If I don't answer him, he'll think I'm crazy, which of course I am after all. Maybe I had better answer him. So here goes with the answer, 'I'm all right, thanks.' Only the answers don't all come out right like that."

He would talk quietly in this way so that after a while I would feel a little as I felt when I was a student at the university and a friendly professor gave me a brief informal lecture on some scientific subject during time off. Sometimes I used to say to myself, "Any man who understands his own condition in this way, cannot be really insane." The next moment my charge would startle me by saying, "See that ship out there, Doctor? Let us go aboard that ship. We will work our passage. We'll go tonight. We'll ask the captain. No, you won't come. You're too proud. All doctors are too proud, that's the trouble with them." Then he would begin to shake with excitement and emotion so that I would have to lead him back to the ward.

Practically all our patients were people without much education. Mr. Smith was a notable exception. It would be wrong to generalize about this, but by and large it seems that the person who is least likely to become insane is the person of more than average intelligence, who has a broad formal or informal education, who reads books, and who is "nervous."

This is my own observation at least and I have my own theory about the matter. The intelligent person is, I believe, better able to cope with what Shakespeare calls "the slings and arrows of outrageous fortune." Most nervous people are intelligent. Their nervousness is often a price they have to pay for their superior mental equipment. If confronted with too great and prolonged adversity, they may go into a state of temporary exhaustion—exactly the same thing as the so-called combat fatigue experienced by fighting men who have been exposed too long to the stress of battle. It never of itself leads to insanity. The nervous person, the chronic worrier, may develop ulcers of the stomach but his mind is likely to remain intact.

We had one patient who was not insane at all—a certain Mr. Mariner. He had been mistakenly admitted to the hospital when he developed hallucinations as the result of a brain tumor, and when the error was discovered he stayed on voluntarily because he had no place to go. He was an intelligent old man. The tumor developed in the pituitary gland and, in growing, it exerted pressure on what is called the optic chiasma, a place where the optic nerves from both eyes come together and then separate again on their way to the back of the brain where the center for vision is located. Pressure on the optic nerves at this point causes disturbances of vision. Mr. Mariner used to see people who were two feet high and whom he called the Kellys. There was another group who were only a foot tall, and these he called the MacDonalds; finally he had a group of friends who were only an inch tall whom he used to call the Smiths, because, he said, they were so numerous. The Smiths were all over the room. They were continually climbing up over him, going in and out of his pockets, hanging on to the buttons of his vest, perching on his shoulder, singing songs he could not hear, standing on tiptoe on the edge of his collar and trying to climb into his ears. They were very real in appearance, he told me, as real as actual people although he was well aware that they were only hallucinations and owed their presence to the tumor which would, before long, cause his death.

He derived a great deal of pleasure from watching the antics of these little people, he said. As he talked, he brushed Smiths from his lapels, picked them off his buttons—gently, of course, so as not to hurt them—and out of his ears. Our apartment was, of course, full of the Smiths. Sometimes the impression he made on us was so strong that some of the little people would remain after he left. . . . Sally will not admit it, but I have caught her, after Mr. Mariner had paid us a visit, brushing off a cookie before eating it and I remember shaking out and inspecting my pajamas very carefully at night before putting them on.

One of my duties was to examine and recommend for discharge any patients who I thought were well enough to go home. If a patient appeared to be doing well, we would hold a meeting consisting of the three medical officers and Mr. Lewison. If it was a female patient the chief nurse on the women's side would replace Mr. Lewison. There was a man called Peter Engels, who I thought should have been discharged long before. He appeared to be perfectly well, emotionally stable and certainly rational in all respects. He was quite a superior type, always very neatly dressed, courteous to everyone, trying to be helpful, cheerful and with a keen sense of humor. I mentioned to Dr. MacEachern several times that I thought he was well enough to be discharged and that we should have him up for conference. Dr. MacEachern was more experienced than I, and he was an extremely careful man—in fact he carried caution almost to a fault—and he was not quite satisfied that Engels was ready to be discharged.

I had many walks with Engels, chatting informally on any subject that might come to mind and noting carefully everything he had to say. I could find nothing wrong. I questioned the attendants regarding his behavior. They said they could not see anything wrong with him and that, in fact, they treated him as one of themselves.

Then one of the attendants added, "He's a great guy. He's always doing something for the other patients. Why, do you know that he will never take a bite of his dinner without giving some of it to Alec first."

For some reason this remark stuck in my mind. That evening during one of our informal chats, when Engels was completely off guard, I asked him a pointed question.

"You have been here quite a long time, Mr. Engels," I said, "longer in fact than I think you should. Do you think you might have any enemies on the outside who might be working to keep you in here?"

He looked at me knowingly.

"On the outside, Doctor? Both on the outside and inside. Not only are they trying to keep me in, but they're trying to poison me. Why, I expect to find cyanide in my food any day."

I did not say anything, nor did he for a moment. Then all of a sudden he started to laugh in a nervous fashion.

"I was only kidding, Doctor, of course I have no enemies. Ha, ha, I was only joking, ha, ha, ha, I hope you didn't fall for it, Doctor."

This man was a paranoid. A paranoid is a person who has a fixed delusion which is "organized." He thinks for example, that a certain person or group of persons want to kill him, and he may decide to kill them first. They are not vague enemies, but are actual specific persons. He "knows" why they want to kill him and takes measures to foil them in their plans. But he is very careful to keep his bizarre notions to himself because he knows they will sound crazy to other people.

This partial insight is what makes the paranoid the most dangerous of all mentally deranged persons. He is able to conceal his lunacy and remains at large in the everyday world. Jack the Ripper was a paranoid, and there have been many other less spectacular criminals who were paranoids. Some of them give themselves away as Engels did by his never failing "kindness" in giving Alec a little taste of his dinner—to check for cyanide—before having any himself; and some may never in their lives cause harm by any overt act. But there are hundreds scattered throughout this great continent who look, act and talk like normal citizens but whose names will, in due time, show up in the crime tabloids.

There is no sure way by which the average person can pick out the person with paranoid tendencies from among his neighbors and it is as well, perhaps, not to worry about it. I have a rule which I think is a good one. If one of my friends plays a mean trick on me he becomes a paranoid and remains one until he does me a good turn. Then he becomes normal. Knowing a little bit about psychiatry is a wonderful advantage.

Unlike the paranoid, the man or woman who attempts suicide cannot conceal the fact of mental illness, though it may of course be no more than a temporary disorder and—if the suicidal person recovers—may be completely cured. I had a hand in helping one such unfortunate, by a slightly unconventional method. Lots of doctors use hypnotism, it is true, but sparingly and with due regard for secrecy. Even today there is something of the weird and strange about it in the minds of most people and no doctor wants to be suspected of being a Rasputin.

However, two years before in Canso, I had *accidentally* hypnotized a young woman, and when Peter Deane was brought to the hospital with his throat slashed and a very strange disability was given as the reason for his act, it eventually occurred to me that what I had done unintentionally might be repeated on purpose to good effect.

My hypnotic subject in Canso had been a woman—actually she was little more than a girl—in labor, under conditions which had thoroughly annoyed me. I had told her that not only would delivery be difficult but the child's life might be endangered, and had exacted a promise from her to go to the hospital in Glasgow when the time came. In this case, at least, poverty did not have to be reckoned with, and as I knew she had a strong wish to stay home, I told her that I refused to have anything to do with her case except at the hospital. In spite of the promises she and her husband had made, she was careful not to call me until the last minute, when it was too late to undertake the journey, knowing very well that I wouldn't, after all, carry out my threat. When I arrived at two o'clock in the morning, I saw through her trick but beyond doing a lot of silent swearing, I had no choice but to do the best I could. Just as I was about to examine her, a pain came and she let out a scream right in my ear. I turned to her quickly and said in a sharp tone, "You keep quiet and go to sleep." To my great surprise she suddenly relaxed and went fast asleep. I proceeded to examine her and she did not stir. In a minute there was another contraction, but still she went on sleeping peacefully. An hour passed before I had delivered the baby. Instruments had to be used and it was a delivery of more than average difficulty. She slept peacefully through it all.

Peter Deane's throat was slashed from ear to ear, but the wound was barely more than skin deep, and although it looked ugly, it was not in any way dangerous. He was a tall thin man who had been a skilled wireless operator on a ship, but who later had retired from this work and was employed in an electrical shop in a small town. He told me that the reason he had tried to do away with himself was that he could not sleep.

It seemed that he had a wife who continually and openly had affairs with other men and who, far from being apologetic for her infidelity, made a practice of taunting him by telling him of these affairs. She used to dare him to do anything about it. Plenty of men have murdered their wives for much less than this, but Peter was not the murdering kind. If there had been only one man involved he could perhaps have searched him out and given him a beating, but apparently his wife's friends were so numerous that to attempt to get after them all would have amounted to starting a small-scale war. He could have divorced her but he had always put it off, although he was continually planning to do so. It is hard to understand how a situation like this could go on for so long. But it happens. Human beings seem to have an almost limitless capacity for endurance.

Peter told the truth when he said that he could not sleep. We tried him with everything we could think of. We gave him Veronal, phenobarbitol, paraldehyde, morphine and almost everything else, with no effect. He would go into a stupor as a result of the drugs but still continued to mumble and toss about and respond to the least sound. We gave him chloral hydrate—a good dose. This is the drug which is used in mixing "Mickey Finns" or "knockout drops" by the operators of dives when they want to render a victim unconscious. It seems to work for them, I am told, but it did not work with Peter. He was haggard and worn from physical exhaustion. On the fourth day I told him I would try giving him an anaesthetic. I put him to bed and gave him chloroform until he was truly unconscious. Twenty minutes after I had stopped the chloroform he was awake again; at least he was thrashing about and talking incoherently.

Hypnosis seemed to be the only thing left. Now hypnotism is very rarely used in mental institutions because, for one thing, mental patients are extremely poor subjects for hypnosis, and there are other reasons as well. It seemed to me, however, that it might be possible to hypnotize Peter, for when not under the influence of drugs he talked in a way that showed considerable intelligence and understanding. At any rate I ordered all drugs discontinued and decided to try the experiment the next day.

Now my knowledge of hypnotism was limited. In medical school the subject had been brushed off very lightly as something of small consequence—rating far less lecture time than whooping cough. I suppose, therefore, that I knew little more about it than the average layman, so I went to the books and read all I could find on the subject. In the *British Encyclopedia of Medical Practice* I found some information; not a great deal, but it was a clear concise article and I absorbed it as well as I was able. I had the books spread out on our living room floor when Sally came in. I told her what I was going to try to do.

"You can do it, dear," she said innocently. "After all you managed to get me here!"

I took my patient into a little room used as an operating room for minor cases, because it was some distance removed from the wards, and quiet. I had him lie down on the operating table, not the most comfortable of couches in spite of the rubber pad, closed the door, and made the room fairly dark by drawing the window shade. I told Peter to keep his eyes fixed on a certain small crack in the ceiling, not directly overhead, but back of the operating table. To watch it he had to keep his eyes almost in the position that would be required if he were trying to look at his own eyebrows. This had the advantage that it was fatiguing to the eyes and therefore required a certain slight effort of the will. It was something to fix his attention on and had the effect of excluding stray rambling thoughts, thereby making his mind receptive to suggestion.

I started to talk to him, trying to make my voice as monotonous as I could. Trying to talk in an even, monotonous tone is not so easy when you are doing something in which you are keenly interested.

"Keep looking at the little crack. Keep looking at it. Keep looking at it. Keep looking at it." I went at this for about two minutes, then, "Your eyes are getting tired. Your eyes are getting tired. Your eyes are getting tired." I could see his upper lids sagging a little. "Keep looking at it, keep looking at it."

Then I started on, "Your eyes are too tired. Your eyes are too tired. Your eyes are too tired. They're closing, they're closing, they're closing. You are going to sleep. You are going to sleep. You are going to sleep. You are asleep, asleep, asleep."

As I repeated, "They're closing," I could see the lids sag and sag until they covered the entire iris. The eyeballs remained in the upward gazing position. Soon only a little line of the white sclera below the iris could be seen. When I started "You are going to sleep," this disappeared altogether. When I had finished repeating "asleep" about a dozen times, I could see his whole body go limp.

"You will sleep until nine o'clock tomorrow; then you will wake up," I said, slowly and clearly.

The next moment he was breathing peacefully and evenly in good sound slumber.

Two orderlies lifted him onto a carriage and wheeled

him off to bed. He actually did sleep until nine o'clock the next morning and then waked up promptly, refreshed and looking like a new man. From that day on he showed a steady improvement in his mental outlook and was discharged a month later. Soon after he left the hospital he obtained a divorce from his wife. I have since heard that he has married again and is apparently perfectly well.

It is obvious from my experience with Peter Deane that it is easy to hypnotize a person who co-operates well and who has faith and confidence. I have also been told that it is impossible for even a skilled hypnotist to put under his spell anyone who is not willing to be hypnotized, and this is generally true, I believe. I have often since used the same words, "You keep quiet and go to sleep," and in pretty much the same tone I used to my Canso patient, when talking to my children, but with them somehow it never seems to have any effect.

Life was very pleasant at the hospital that summer. I threw myself into the study of mental diseases in good earnest. I fancied that a knowledge of psychiatry would at least be no burden to carry later on when I came to brain surgery, even though the two are very separate fields. Study, when it is not undertaken under pressure, can be the most soothing of occupations.

We had plenty of company—members of the medical, nursing and business staffs, friends in Halifax and Sally's sister, Mary, who worked in the city as a secretary. On our days off we sometimes went to the city, but more often we spent our time at a beach on a small cove called Cow Bay, just outside the entrance of Halifax harbor. Here there was sand to lie on, the Atlantic Ocean to look at or swim in, and *peace*. On days off we could go swimming or for little trips about the countryside. Our immediate causes for worry were temporarily suspended. Our living was provided for us and we were able to send to our creditors each month, very small amounts of money which had the effect of giving their letter writers a rest—what a relief it must have been for them! We no longer feared to open the day's mail and the two little Penguin volumes of *The Worst Journey in the World* lay neglected on a shelf.

Sally was busy all the time. I don't know how she contrived to find so much to do in a place where the last detail of housekeeping was looked after for us and did not even require direction. She used to go looking for imaginary dust, I think. A lot of the activity, of course, had to do with the event which we expected in December. This now became our number one topic of discussion. I suppose we spent at least three hours out of every twenty-four talking about it. Multiply three by two-hundred and eighty and you have eight hundred and forty hours of discussion and planning. I am sure the D-Day invasion was planned in fewer hours than that! Almost every evening when we were alone our conversation would run something like this:

"Let's talk about something else tonight for a change."

"Yes, let's. We'll talk about books or music or something."

There would be silence for a minute and then—

"Speaking of books, I wonder why that new book on Child Care we sent for hasn't come yet." Or, "Speaking of music, I suppose we will have to move the radio into the other living room, after he comes."

It was always "he" now—at first it had been "it."

If we started to talk about a movie we had seen, we wouldn't be on the subject two minutes, when Sally would say, "You would never think to look at her" (the movie heroine) "that she has two children."

No matter how the conversation began it would turn out the same way. Once I got out *The Worst Journey* again and Sally said, "Wouldn't it be awful to have to have a baby down at the South Pole!"

Sally had told the news only to one or two of her women friends, but it was not very many weeks before everybody knew, including, of course, all the patients. When we took walks about the grounds in the evenings the parolees used to greet us with warm friendly smiles. Some of them took a great personal interest in the coming event. One patient, an old-timer of some thirty years in the institution, saved up money to buy a present—a blue blanket—for the baby. He earned the money in an odd way. The tunnels which linked the various buildings, together, and some old disused parts of the ancient cellars, were infested with rats and, for patients who liked to spend an hour or two a day in subterranean hunting, there was a bounty of five cents on each rat tail. Some of the parolees did quite well at this for a time, until the bounty was withdrawn because a racket developed. They started "hi-jack-ing" rat tails from one another.

Something about which we thought a good deal was the question of what to do when the year would be up. We tried to school ourselves not to think about it too much but we only partially succeeded. I remember trying to dream up fantastic ideas for acquiring a lot of money in a short time. For example, I thought of writing a short story, one that could be done in three or four days and yet be so terrific that it would sell for thousands of dollars. I invented some very good plots and titles, but somehow by the time I got out the bridge table, set the typewriter on it and put a sheet of paper in place, the idea always seemed to go stale. After seeing the picture *Lost Horizon,* I tried to think up a story which would be just like Mr.

Hilton's, yet totally different and original and even better. If I could have done it I'm sure we would have made lots of money.

On the other hand, Sally sent a recipe in to the New York *Sunday News* and won five dollars for it. We will never forget the day the recipe appeared in that big New York paper, with her name over it. Think of it! Her name, our name, splashed all over the world! I told her that perhaps at that very minute Franklin D. Roosevelt or Clark Gable was trying one of her cocoanut macaroons and she told me I was crazy; but she was pleased just the same.

Chapter Ten

O UR baby was born on December 16 at the Halifax
Infirmary. I remember that I saw him when he was only
two minutes old. At least I kind of saw him, but it was
like looking through three pairs of glasses all belonging
to somebody else, and I thought he looked like the most
pitiful baby I had ever seen. His nose was flattened and
he had deep dents on either side of his head. I felt sorry
for Sally. She would be heartbroken, I knew. Two days
later when his face had bounced back into shape, and I
had the three pairs of glasses off, I saw that he was the most
beautiful baby in the world. I saw him that day through
the big window in the nursery. Sally's sister, Mary, was
with me. He was in his crib, sleeping, and as we watched

he moved one little arm. We both started and said to each other, "Look, he moved his arm!"

It is a curious thing about babies. They exist for the greater part of a year almost as nuisances, and certainly as physical encumbrances, and then, all of a sudden, the moment they are born they become worth a million dollars. Pound for pound they exert far more influence and power than father and mother put together—and not only in the home. The influence of one squalling, soft-nosed, bottle-sucking, cute little dictator may extend over nations and even alter the course of history. If Helen of Troy, for example, had had a baby she wouldn't have had time to launch those thousand ships and cause a war. She would have been too busy changing diapers. If a brand-new baby had walked into Napoleon's tent, the history of Europe might have been quite different. Nearly all the trouble in the world is caused by people who have no babies or at least not enough of them. It would be easy to prove if one took the time.

When Sally came home we installed our particular little valuable creature in a special room equipped as a nursery. The furniture in this nursery deserves special mention. It was not made in Grand Rapids, Michigan, or in England. They wouldn't have been up to it in those places. They don't know enough. It was made by four of our patient friends in the hospital—inmates, men of unsound mind, perhaps, but of sound heart.

Among the parolees there were two men who had been master craftsmen at cabinetmaking before they had become sick; and when word had spread among the patients that we were expecting a new baby, they had gone to Mr. McInnis, chief engineer at the hospital, and asked to be allowed to make some furniture for us. Mr. McInnis was a good friend of ours and he knew our circumstances, so he approved of the idea. He gave them the use of the hospital workshop, where they had done some things for him before, and gave them access to the necessary materials. They worked like beavers for more than a month and in the end produced a crib, a clothes cabinet and a table, all of the finest workmanship I have ever seen, polished and smoothed and complete in every last detail. Another patient made the spring for the crib by laboriously taking apart a spring from an old discarded hospital bed and knitting each wire together onto an angle-iron framework. Still another painted the furniture, spending days on it and making it look beautiful.

Some days after the nursery had been taken over by Ronnie—perhaps a hundred hours of discussion and argument had gone into the selection of this name—we had our furniture-making friends in to see him. They were very proud. After they had admired sufficiently, mostly in silence because they were not men who were given to talking very much, they had supper with us. We had candles on the table and for each there was a little glass of wine, and the best food that the hospital kitchen could turn out—which was very good indeed. The candlelight shone on faces that were wrinkled and marked with the imprint of years of loneliness and separation from normal human contact. I could not read from their faces what their thoughts were as they sat down to a table with candles and white linen and silver, they who had been so long away from family life. Perhaps they had memories of long ago, of a time when the world about them had been real and solid and not just a weirdly distorted picture.

January came bringing snow and storms. It was a happy quiet month in our little private world. Ronnie thrived with the energy of a young bear cub and watching him grow we forgot about the approaching end of our term.

The patients were happy. Mental patients are at their best in stormy weather, more quiet and peaceful and less apt to lapse into violent moods than during continued calm weather. February brought extreme cold—the thermometer outside our window hovered between twenty and twenty-eight below zero for weeks—and then March came and with it brief thaws and other signs of approaching spring. March indicated that it was time for us to return to our worrying sessions. We had two more months in which to solve the problem of what to do next. The end of our year's contract was approaching.

From some points of view, ours was an ideal life. The work was light, we had regular hours—a luxury to any doctor, we had a comfortable home and good food with no worries about rent, grocery bills, and so on. Each month our salary was divided like a pie into a great many small portions and mailed out to some twenty or more creditors. All very pleasant indeed, but we knew it was only an interlude. Even if we had wanted to renew our contract, we could not have stayed on for several reasons. First of all, the salary was too small. Secondly, I was doing very little actual medical work, my duties being more administrative than anything else, and therefore it was inevitable that, as a doctor, I should find myself slipping if this continued much longer. With my two chiefs and colleagues it was a different matter. They were interested in psychiatry first and last. But there was a reason that transcended both of these.

It was now almost three years since I had set out from medical school on a road which I thought would lead me to a specific goal. Time and again I had been pushed back, so that now I was much farther away from it than on the day I had so blithely started out. Each time I had been flattened down by Fate, so to speak, I had come up to find the star of my ambition blazing more brightly than ever. It was not heroic determination on my part that was responsible, it was simply a reaction to frustration. The desire to be a brain surgeon had grown to be an obsession with me. I could not hear mention of Cushing or Penfield without a pang of envy. A great impatience seized me. Money! We had to get some, somewhere, somehow; nothing could be more clear and certain than this. I almost wished I hadn't been brought up with so many scruples about such things as, say, robbing banks. I think I would have tried it.

Towards the end of March we began to write letters again and to seek information from every possible source regarding a place in which to practice. In April we received a letter from a doctor in Digby County in which he stated that he wanted someone to relieve him for a month while he went on vacation. This was not what we wanted but we felt that we should not overlook anything, so we decided to go to see him, on the off chance that something more worthwhile would come of it. This western end of the province was unexplored territory to us and we thought we should look into it.

We made arrangements with Mary to look after Ronnie for a weekend and on a Saturday morning we headed in the direction of Digby, about one hundred and fifty miles away.

As we were leaving, Sally said, "Do you know what?"

"No, what?"

"I have an itchy left palm."

"Well," I said, "is that anything to be excited about?"

"It means this trip is going to mean something good for us. We're going to get money."

"How much money?" I asked.

"How do I know?" she answered. "But you wait and see."

"Hmn, ridiculous!" I said, but for some reason I felt more cheerful.

It was a pleasant day for driving and by midafternoon we were in Digby. That evening we had a talk with Dr. Wise whom we had come to see.

Dr. Wise was a serious, agreeable, middle-aged man. He ld us about his practice, which apparently was a busy one, and about the type of population he served. He asked us some questions about ourselves and we told him some of our story. He was very much interested.

During dinner he said, "They tell me Dr. Damien is going away."

I asked who and where Dr. Damien was.

"He's in Little Brook," he said. "He's had a fine practice there and I know he has done well; I think he's been working too hard. At any rate he's leaving to study Eye, Ear, Nose and Throat work. It seems to me that that should be a good place."

That night in the hotel I tried to reach Dr. Damien by telephone only to find that he had already left and was on his way to England where he was to take up his special studies. I managed to talk to his wife, however, and what she told me was more than enough to get Sally and me excited. It was a wonderful practice, she said; the people were wonderful and they were badly in need of a doctor now her husband was gone.

We were elated, although I tried to look casual and even bored with the prospect. I went so far as to tilt back my head and look at my fingernails after the fashion of a top-flight movie gangster ordering a few residents of Chicago to be "rubbed out." Sally didn't need to act. She simply sat with a self-satisfied, almost smug look on her face.

"There now, what did I tell you about that itchy palm?"

We went to see Little Brook the next day. It was only a brief visit because we had to be back at our post that night, and we carried away only the haziest impressions of a little village with white painted houses, a few stores and a church, all hugging the shore of the Bay of Fundy. We talked to Mrs. Damien and were impressed by her charm and sincerity. We left with a feeling that immense good fortune had come to us, eager for the moment when we could come here to live. After all, in our circumstances, it was an easy decision to make. We were in high spirits that evening when we got home to our baby.

It was not many days after this that something occurred which caused us to make a slight revision in our plans. The annual meeting of the Nova Scotia Medical Society was held in Halifax that year. Like any convention, such a gathering usually lasts three or four days and is held in a large hotel. You listen to lectures by imported speakers, prominent medical men from other cities, for about five hours a day, and there are luncheons and social events of various kinds. I had not attended a proper medical meeting in the last year so I decided to attend this one, and to take Sally to some of the luncheons scheduled for wives of visiting doctors.

The first day I attended all the lectures faithfully, and I was slightly disturbed to find that I was hearing quite a few things that were new to me. Can it be, I thought, that I have slipped that much in only one year away from general practice? I reproached myself for not having read the medical journals more faithfully. A luncheon was to be held, at the end of the first day's lecture session, and before the luncheon there was the usual adjournment to the lounge just off the dining room, in which a temporary cocktail bar had been set up. Here everybody gathered in little groups, sipping cocktails and discussing the only things that doctors ever talk about when they are together. Everyone was trying to make his fellow doctor listen to the case he had "one time," and the fellow doctor was trying to tell about the more spectacular case *he* had. These talks had always been a joy to me before, but today there was something wrong. I found myself with no case to talk about. I listened to a conversation that went something like this:

"Have you heard that Moore finds that the incidence of hyperostosis frontalis is 0.014?"

"Sure. Brule is using Para-amino-phenyl-sulfamide for the treatment of diplococcic arthritis."

"Yes, I know. They tell me that Fenz and Zell are producing cholesterol reduction in rabbits by injecting di-iodotyrosine."

My heart went down in my boots. I had never even heard of Para-amino-phenyl-sulfamide before and I was doubtful about hyperostosis frontalis. I felt as if I had just had a good dose of di-iodotyrosine, and my cholesterol was down to zero. I wondered if I had really ever gone to medical school and if so, why they had let me graduate. In the group next to me I heard someone say something about short wave irradiation for hypogalactia. That sounded like astronomy to me. I wondered if I had by accident blundered into the wrong convention. I decided to go find Sally.

"Dear," I said to her, "your husband is a has-been. You are free to leave me if you want to, and go home to your mother. I cannot expect you to remain the wife of an ignorant quack doctor in sheep's clothing. Imagine, the only word I recognized in all that talk was the word 'rabbit.' "

"And how many cocktails did you have?" she asked.

That evening we had a serious talk. The science of medicine moves ahead so rapidly that to be out of it even for one year leaves you at a disadvantage. Now we were going back to it I thought we should brush up a little before starting general practice again. The answer was to take a short post-graduate course.

We looked up the notices in the *Journal of the Canadian Medical Association* and found that while excellent courses were given in Montreal and Toronto, there were none running just at the particular time that we wanted. Most of these short courses are given in the fall and winter. We thought a while and then the answer occurred to us. There is one city in the world in which you can get anything you want, and exactly when you want it—that is New York. We looked up the *Journal of the American Medical Association,* and sure enough we found the notices we had been looking for. The New Yorkers were willing to teach us anything we wanted to know, and at any time we wanted to go there. We picked on the New York Post-Graduate Hospital as the place and the fifteenth of May as the time.

It was on a very fine morning that we started off for New York. We had left Ronnie, who was now five months old, in charge of Sally's parents. Our little green Austin Seven, the smallest of the Austin family, was far from being new. It could go as fast as forty-five miles an hour on the level with a favorable wind, about thirty-five miles an hour if the wind was against us. It had a four-speed-forward gearshift and this was in use almost all the time. Steering was a trick business if there happened to be a cross wind blowing. Even the draught caused by another car passing at high speed caused our little car to swerve and had to be compensated for by a twist of the steering wheel. This might not seem like an ideal vehicle with which to start a thousand-mile journey, but as the event proved, it was better for us than a Cadillac would have been.

We carried with us, besides our personal effects, a large carton in which we had a frying pan, kettle, saucepan for cooking potatoes, knives and forks and cups and saucers. We also had a small stock of groceries and it was our intention to prepare meals on the roadside rather than to patronize restaurants.

Starting out on a long journey is always an exhilarating experience, especially if you are heading for a large and famous city for the first time. But we had gone only twenty miles on our way when something went wrong with the car engine. There was a cough, a catch, more coughs and then the car stopped. From past experience I knew what was wrong. I lifted the hood, got out some tools and unscrewed the gas line where it entered the carburetor. Sally went to the back of the car, took the cover off the gas tank and put her ear to it. Then I put my mouth to the end of the copper tube and blew. In a minute Sally called out that she could hear the air bubbling up through the tank. Then I knew the line was clear and I screwed the tube back in place again. We got back into the car and started off once more. Sally said, "How many times does twenty go into a thousand?"

"Fifty times," I said.

"Oh, well," she said, "I suppose it's worth it."

The next afternoon we were at the American border between the towns of St. Stephen, on the Canadian side, and Calais, on the American side. A few miles before coming to the border, we had stopped and I had taken the green cross medical emblems off the front and back of the car and hidden them away under the seat. We did not want to give the American customs officials a poor opinion of the Canadian medical profession. We also took our carton of cooking utensils and groceries and put them at the bottom of our heap of luggage hoping that they would neglect to examine it. We tidied ourselves up as best we could. It was our hope that the Immigration and Customs people would take us for a holiday couple who drove a small car like this just for the fun of the thing, and who probably had a Buick in the garage at home. We had heard of wealthy people doing such things and we braced ourselves to look very nonchalant as we drove up to the American side and were signaled to stop by a uniformed official.

They were very courteous, these uniformed guardians of the United States of America, but, on this day at least, they were very thorough. They not only went through all our luggage, but they also took out and put on the examining rack our cardboard box, and turned over the frying pan, the kettle and looked around among the groceries. I felt sick when they asked me to unwrap a small wax-paper package containing three strips of dry, cooked bacon and a cold fried egg. There were other cars standing there at the same time and we felt that everybody was staring at us. We did our best to look casual. Finally the inspection was finished and they waved to us to move ahead. With great relief we got back into the car and I stepped on the starter. There was a whirring noise but the engine did not start. I tried again with the same result. We looked at each other. Would we have to go into our routine here, of all places? I kept spinning the starter. Finally we knew there was no help for it. With very red faces, we got out of the car, I lifted the hood and Sally went to the back and took the cap off the gas tank. Nobody laughed, out loud at least.

We got going again and after a while, rolling along the highways of Maine, we gradually forgot our humiliation in the absorption of seeing new things. Soon we were remarking to each other that Maine had spruce trees that appeared to be just the same as the ones in Canada, that the grass was more or less of the same shade of green and not purple or pink, and that it was certainly wonderful to be able to buy gasoline for twenty cents a gallon.

We got to New York on the evening of the fourth day. It was Sunday and for the last thirty miles the highway was jammed with cars, driving bumper to bumper in four streams. We were exhausted from the long day on the road and the noise and confusion. We had the naive notion that we would be able—when we got into Manhattan —to drive straight to the New York Post-Graduate Hospital, find a rooming house near by, and get all settled right away. From the moment we passed New Rochelle we were helpless in the stream of traffic. We did not know that in order to turn right we must first get into an outside lane and to turn left we must be on an inside lane. We were caught in the stream of traffic and stayed there— unable to turn right or left, or even to stop.

It was now about nine o'clock. The first thing we knew we were being swept onto the George Washington Bridge and saw signs that told us we were leaving Manhattan and going into New Jersey and that we would have to pay a fifty cent toll. We did not want to go to New Jersey and certainly did not want to pay fifty cents, but we had no choice—the stream of automobiles swept us along. We also saw another sign that said "Minimum Speed 40 miles per Hour." We were so busy trying to make this minimum speed, which was almost the maximum for our little car, that we gave up thinking of where we were going. Our sole ambition now was to get out of that fast procession and stop. Finally we saw our chance. A long piece ahead we could see that there was an intersection. I took a firm grip on the wheel and got set. When we reached the intersection, without slowing up—I was afraid to slow up—we swung sharply to the right, making the turn almost on two wheels, and in a few minutes were in the calm waters of Teaneck, New Jersey. Just then the back left tire went flat and we pulled up at the curb on a quiet and darkened street.

We were now dead tired and our only thought was to find a place to sleep. We started to tramp the streets looking for a rooming house. We stopped people and asked questions. There were very few rooming houses in the vicinity, but we found them and rang doorbells. In every place we heard the same story—no vacancies. There was a circus in the neighborhood, it appeared, and all rooms were taken. There were no hotels in Teaneck, we were told; we would have to go back to Manhattan. Rather than venture back into that roaring tumult that night, we would have slept on the ground. We walked the streets for hours, stopping now and then to sit on the curb to rest for a few minutes.

A young colored boy pointed out a house on a side street where, he said, they sometimes took roomers. The place was in complete darkness. We rang the doorbell again and again with no result. With the aid of a flashlight we saw that around the side of the house there was a semi-horizontal door which apparently led into a basement. We tried it and it was unlocked. We went down some stone steps, pushed our way among some empty boxes and barrels and found a flight of stairs leading to the floor above. We started up. We were housebreaking and we knew it. If there was anyone at the top of those stairs they had a perfect right to shoot us. We thought of that but it didn't seem to make any difference. We opened a door at the head of the stairs and found ourselves in a lighted kitchen where two people, a man and a woman, sat at a table with a bottle between them.

They were the most villainous-looking people we had ever seen and they were both very drunk. They looked at us in a dazed way when they saw us but they did not seem to be very excited at our unusual entry into their house.

"You circus people?" asked the man in an unsteady voice.

"Yes," I said, thinking it better not to let him know that we were complete strangers in a foreign land, "and we need a room for the night."

They whispered something to each other. Then the man looked me up and down.

"Pretty husky fellow, ain't you," he said. I was wearing a heavy red sweater and under it I had the sleeves of my thick khaki shirt rolled up high—a habit of mine. This, I suppose, gave an illusion of bulging muscles. I tried to smile in a careless way, as I imagined a circus strong man might do. They conferred again, and then the woman said, "All right, I guess we can give you a room."

She got up and lead the way to a room on the second floor. We were surprised to find that the place was quite clean. As soon as we had closed the door and we heard the woman walking unsteadily down the stairs, Sally said, "Quick, let's pile everything we can against the door. They look like very desperate people." There was a chest of drawers and two chairs in the room besides the bed. These we moved over to the door. We carried the chest of drawers instead of pushing it, although it was very heavy, so as not to make any noise. Then we sat on the edge of the bed and smoked a cigarette and talked in whispers to each other. We decided that the safest thing would be to take turn about sleeping so there would be one of us on guard all the time. We tried to do this but somehow we both fell fast alseep. The next thing we knew it was daylight.

When we had got dressed and washed we came downstairs and found that the villainous-looking man and woman had disappeared. In their place was a harmless middle-aged couple, looking a little bleary-eyed from a night's drinking, but quite friendly. It was hard to believe they were the same people. They gave us instructions about getting back into the city. It was a bright fine day. Soon a cheerful garage man was fixing our tire and we were having a good breakfast in a corner cafeteria. The world looked wonderful again.

The New York Post-Graduate Hospital was to me an amazing place, principally on account of the volume of work done. I soon met Dr. Erdmann, who was surgeon-in-chief, a most remarkable man. There may be better general surgeons in the world than Dr. Erdmann but there cannot be many. About seventy years old, white-haired, wiry and as full of energy as a man of twenty, he was perhaps the busiest and most active man on the staff. All morning long he performed feats of surgical wizardry. He could work so fast that he could do in fifteen minutes an operation on which an ordinary good surgeon would spend an hour. I saw him do an abdominal hysterectomy—removal of the uterus or womb—in five minutes, and yet it was done without any appearance of haste and with great neatness and precision. Every part was clearly exposed. Every major artery stood clear, pulsating, before he put a clamp on it. There was little or no blood to obscure vision. Everything stood out as clearly as in a diagram even to us, who observed from a distance of about eight or ten feet.

It is not, of course, this technical skill and speed that makes a good surgeon. Some men who are skilled with their hands are not good surgeons and should not be allowed near the operating room. Other men who are very slow operators are very excellent surgeons. There are two things which are more important than technical skill—diagnostic ability and good surgical judgment. Dr. Erdmann had both in addition to his uncanny technical ability.

There is one other quality which is of great importance in making a good doctor in any branch of medicine, and that is "heart," or feeling for the patient. God help the patients who fall into the hands of a man who has not this! If their illnesses happen to be of a well-defined nature so that only one clear course of treatment is warranted, then they will not be so badly off. But in practice very many cases are not so clear and the patient is at the mercy of any scientific whim the surgeon may have—and there are such things as scientific whims! In general, if a patient knows from long association that a certain doctor is a man of integrity and has his best interests at heart, he should be loath to run off to a "big-name" man or group of men whose only interest in him may consist of wondering what the autopsy will show. I think most of our high-ranking surgeons are like Dr. Erdmann and consider the patient as a human being and not merely as an object of scientific study but, shocking as this may seem, there are some who are not.

There was the case of Margaret, an attractive young girl of nineteen, doomed to die because she had a certain malformation of an internal organ which up until a very few years ago could not be cured or corrected by operation. However, now two or three famous surgeons were operating successfully upon this kind of condition. Margaret went to her family doctor who himself happened to be quite a famous internist. The doctor got in touch with Dr. X who was one of the men doing this type of operation. Dr. X refused to have anything to do with the case on the grounds that Margaret was a poorer risk than usual because of her age and he *did not want to take a chance on spoiling his series of cases!* Fortunately the family doctor was able to get one of the other surgeons to do it and Margaret lived. This did not happen in New York.

Another example which illustrates the way of thinking of the ultra-scientific type of mind is that of Alex Williams, an old man who was receiving treatment for a minor condition in a hospital one day, when all of a sudden his heart stopped beating. This is not an uncommon event, of course, among aged people, but it happened that a bright and energetic young intern was present. This young man promptly got hold of a syringe, a long needle, and ten minims of adrenalin which he quickly injected directly into the poor old heart. The heart started to beat again, the man lived and was in due time discharged from the hospital. The young intern was congratulated by everybody including his chief. A few days later at a conference at which about fifty doctors were present, this case was one of those brought up for discussion. The chief-of-staff talked a few minutes about the case and again he commended the intern for his alertness, but, he added in conclusion, "I do not recommend this procedure of injecting the heart. In the first place it is very seldom effective, and in the second place it spoils the heart for autopsy." It is to the credit of the medical profession in general that a gasp of horror was audible throughout the auditorium.

Seeing Dr. Erdmann at work made me feel like a hopeless amateur who should never be allowed inside an operating room except, perhaps, to fix the plumbing. Fortunately for my morale I also saw dozens of other men at work, good competent surgeons who did excellent work but who were less spectacular. Seeing and talking to these men, I took heart again.

Operations at the NYPG were of all types. With half a dozen operating rooms, all busy at once, there was an endless variety of things to see. I watched an operation for the repair of a cleft palate. A baby was brought in, already under anaesthetic, so small that it looked like a rabbit, and wrapped around snugly with cloth so that only the head was moveable. The tiny mouth was kept open by a special type of mouth gag and after the preliminary draping and other preparation, the surgeon started to work. He made an incision on each side of the palate, near the gum line, and then using a small chisel-like instrument proceeded to separate the mucous membrane from the palate bone. This was to loosen or free it so that the soft tissues could be pulled together in the center to close the defect. After he had finished this and cut a very thin strip from each of the opposing edges of the defect he began putting in a great number of sutures. The problem in these cases is to keep the tissues joined together long enough for them to heal. Because of the ever-present germ population of the mouth and the complete impossibility of keeping it sterile, pus forms, preventing proper healing, and the tension on the soft tissues often pulls the edges apart when the sutures are removed. It is meticulous and painstaking work and only to be undertaken by specialists. Today, with drugs like penicillin so freely used, infection is very much decreased and these operations are much more often successful.

I was on the alert to see some surgery of the brain. In my internship years I had watched teaching films depicting operations of this type, but I had yet to see an actual case. Now I had an opportunity to watch some of this work at first hand, and I was not slow to seize it. It was a source of wonder to me with what coolness and self-assurance—I will not say "carefree abandon" although the phrase comes to mind—the surgeons opened that sacred box called the skull. They drilled holes and made little doors in it to expose to view the most complicated mechanism known to man. Viewed directly with the naked eye, the brain is a gray-white indeterminate sort of mass. It has no moving parts like the heart or intestines. It has no outstanding features that catch the eye. Yet it is without doubt the most wonderful thing that the eye of man can see.

Watching such an operation is not very interesting to most doctors. It is an endless repetition of small movements on the part of the operator and is tedious to everyone except the operator himself. But I was spellbound. It is amazing how the brain can be pierced by instruments that look like ice picks, singed with electric currents, cut and hacked with knives and mutilated in general without leaving any gross ill effects. There is the classic case of the workman who was tamping down blasting powder in a small hole with a crowbar when the charge went off. The crowbar in its entire length passed through the front part of his brain, entering through the eye socket and emerging through the top of his skull. Incredible as it may seem, he not only recovered, but was—except for the loss of one eye—apparently normal in all respects. The front part of his brain had been literally scattered in all directions, yet he could talk, think, move about and do everything that he had done before. The well-known and accurately charted areas which control speech, hearing, vision, motion, receive sensation and hold certain types of memory, are not located in the front part of the brain, and had not been damaged.

But what is the function of the large *uncharted* areas of the brain? What mysterious things lie there, awaiting discovery? We have vague intriguing hints, but we do not know.

During our free time—Sally did some nursing at the NYPG—we wandered all over the city. We found Pete's Tavern near Gramercy Park where O. Henry used to go, and drank ale and talked with Tim, the waiter, who became our friend. We stuck our noses inside a night club, just to be able to say we had been there, and we saw *Tobacco Road,* then in the fourth year of its run, but our budget made it necessary to learn more about the "free" entertainment New York offers than most visitors ever know. All the city was a show, for us, and a seat on a bus was as good as the front row in any theatre.

We visited Wall Street which is so famous that there is hardly an Eskimo in Labrador or a monk in Tibet who has not lost money there. We had ourselves contributed thirty-nine dollars to it once upon a time, which gave us a sort of personal interest in the place. Now we stood on the steps of J. P. Morgan and Co. and several millionaires brushed by us and one of them asked me for a light. Another millionaire who was not as busy as the rest paused on our step for a moment before going down the street, and said it was a fine day. I said it certainly was—always being anxious to agree with millionaires. Sally said that these men were likely only clerks and calendar salesmen and electrical repairmen and so on, but I refused to believe her. We also saw some millionaire's daughters coming out of the building. They were disguised to look like stenographers and they fooled Sally completely, but I could see through the disguises right away. Sometimes Sally is a little dumb. Like the day we were in the Metropole Bar and saw Walter Winchell. Just because he did not look exactly the way he does in the pictures, she insisted it was not he.

We got acquainted with the Bowery and Greenwich Village and the parks and Fifth Avenue. In two afternoons we walked the entire length of Broadway—or at least from Battery Park to 145th Street. Everywhere people we met were anxious to talk to us, to show us the way and to point out this or that place of interest. I do not understand people who think that New Yorkers are cold and indifferent. A few may be so busy and preoccupied that they have no time to spend talking to strangers or to each other for that matter, but I have known people like that in the very smallest towns and villages.

Chapter Eleven

AFTER two months we turned the nose of our little Austin towards home, where we found Ronnie safe and well. He had not been kidnaped, had not got pneumonia, and had not wasted away to nothing, pining for us. On the contrary he was not only fat and healthy but he hardly seemed to care at all that we had been away. Sally had to start at once to recapture his affections from Sissie, her younger sister. We spent a few days with Sally's parents and telling stories about New York. The stories were only partly exaggerated—you cannot exaggerate New York—but we managed to give them the impression that our room on Twentieth Street near Second Avenue was in one of the more fashionable residential districts, and by mentioning certain better-class restaurants and hotels that we had passed by once or twice we more or less led them to understand that we had been living pretty well.

I left Sally and Ronnie and went to Little Brook to make final arrangements. The first person I met was Dr. Phillip Saulnier, a dentist. He was a stocky young man of about medium height, dark-complexioned, with a belligerent expression which was deceiving until one came to know him. He told me immediately that Little Brook needed a doctor very badly indeed. There was such a lot of work he said, that the previous doctor had been kept so busy he had had to give up from sheer fatigue, after working almost twenty-four hours a day for about ten years.

At once I was suspicious. I had had plenty of experience at working twenty-four hours a day and it had brought me into worse than bankruptcy. I hated to bring up the question of money as I did not want him to think that I was mercenary, but the few dollars I had in my pocket were borrowed and the letters from the creditors were becoming disagreeable again. But he assured me that there was no need for worry on this score. The people, he said, had money and were very faithful about paying their bills.

He suggested that we start to practice as soon as possible. He even knew of a nine-room house we could get, which had been built only four years ago and had never been occupied. He thought we could rent it at a reasonable price. He would take me to see the owner right away.

Before we left he took me into another part of the house in which he had his office and introduced me to his father and mother, Mr. and Mrs. Moise Saulnier. Moise was a farmer, with a face rugged and lined and tanned by long exposure to sun and wind. He would have made a good subject for a painter. Mrs. Moise, too, I liked immediately. She had lived in the United States a long time and spoke with a wonderful mixture of accents, part Boston, part Pennsylvania and part French. She was a cheerful woman and very good-hearted. During the next few years we were to come to know her and Moise very well and to respect them deeply.

Then we went to see Emil Comeau, a middle-aged bachelor who lived with his brother directly across the street from the house which I wanted to rent and which he owned. He told me that the house was not wired for electricity and that there was no plumbing, although there was a very good well in the basement which he had dug and lined and cemented himself before starting to build the place. If I was willing to put in the electricity and plumbing, I could have the house. I asked him about the price. He reflected a few minutes, and then said, in a hesitating manner, "Would five dollars a month be too much?"

I thought he must mean five dollars a week. Pretending I hadn't heard clearly, I asked him to repeat.

"Five dollars a month," he said again, apologetically.

"Well," I said slowly, trying to be casual but all the time feeling like a robber, "I think that would be all right." We found out afterward that most people who paid rent in the area paid about four dollars a month. We knew one couple who rented a completely furnished house with every modern convenience for four dollars a month.

This was only the first of a series of surprises in store for us—the first hint that we had stumbled into one of the most amazing communities in the world, even better than the fictional Shangri-La because this one was real.

After a few days rest with Sally's parents, we loaded up the little car one morning with as many of our personal possessions as it would hold. The back part was packed to the ceiling. On the little luggage rack at the rear we piled suitcases, and cartons and everything we could, and tied them on as well as possible with clothesline. On the roof we put the playpen and other things that could stand exposure to weather. When we had finished there was just exactly room for Sally, me and the baby in the front seat, and nothing to spare, and by late afternoon of the second day we were crossing the boundaries of the district in which we were to practice.

For some reason I had not, during my first two brief visits, noticed that the place differed very much in appearance from other rural villages in Nova Scotia, but this time as we drove the last ten miles or so we saw a few things which came as a jolt. It was a fine day and men were working in the fields—and they were using, not tractors, not horses, but oxen. We had never seen oxen used before. When we saw the first pair Sally said, "Oh, look at that poor farmer. I suppose he can't afford to buy a horse."

We passed the next farm and the next. Everywhere we saw oxen, walking at what seemed to be about one mile per hour and men with short sticks walking beside them just as slowly. Nowhere was a horse to be seen.

What a backward, primitive people, we thought. Again we saw a number of people on bicycles, not only children, but middle-aged and even elderly people.

"They are still in the bicycle age," we said to each other. "This is as high as they have come in modern civilization." Although I did not say it aloud, the thought struck me that perhaps we were on a wrong track again. How could we make a living, to say nothing of paying our debts and saving money in this land of ox-carts and bicycles?

We passed a lot of shiny automobiles, too, a good proportion of them in the higher-price class, but we took it for granted that these were driven by people from the outside world just passing through. Not for a minute did we associate the men who walked beside the oxen with Buicks and Oldsmobiles; these poor plodding farmers must envy us our little green Austin, and look up to us as "city slickers" because we owned a car.

We arrived at our new home and found that in the few days since I had been here before, the "poor primitive" electrician and plumber I had engaged had completely wired the place and installed a modern water system and bathroom with an efficiency that would have put Mr. Henry Kaiser to shame.

We inspected the house, the three of us hand in hand. It had nine rooms, not counting the bathroom and a large back place intended for firewood. The plaster was white and unmarked, the woodwork unscored, the floors bare but spotless. Everything about it was simple and, of course, except for a bed and four plain kitchen chairs for which I had arranged, it was bare of any furniture; but it was spotlessly clean and I could see that Sally was pleased.

The ancient stove with oven on top, which I had bought for ten dollars on my first trip, had been set up by our landlord and there was firewood which he had thoughtfully provided. We made a fire and then I started to unload the car. We set up Ronnie's crib and playpen, Sally unpacked the cartons which contained the dishes and cooking things, and in a short while the kettle was singing and the teapot was warming on the stove. Sally was enjoying the thrill of planning what rooms she would use for this or that purpose and making remarks on the uninteresting subject of curtains, when the kitchen door opened and we heard a breezy hail. Our first callers, Dr. Phillip and Mr. and Mrs. Moise, brought with them jars of home-preserved venison, pickles, a loaf of fresh homemade bread and a hot meatpie, just out of the oven.

"There are a few little ways and customs around here that may seem rather strange at first," Dr. Phillip said as they were leaving. "But there are worse places in the world."

When we went upstairs we could see out the window a clear moonlight night and the bay in front of us, and the road and little pinpoints of light stretching away for miles.

"We're going to learn the sequel to an old story here," said Sally thoughtfully.

"What do you mean?" I asked.

"I mean that these people are the descendants of Evangeline or her sisters—because Evangeline didn't get married. It's too bad Longfellow can't come back and write another poem."

Most people know the story of Evangeline; of how nearly seven thousand people were suddenly and violently plucked from their homes and from their fields and carried away in prison ships to be scattered haphazardly along the Atlantic coast from Massachusetts to South Carolina. In that terrible episode thousands perished, dying of cold, starvation and disease. But a few survived in spite of everything. Of these some eventually made their way back to the land of their birth. One group, numbering about nine hundred, had made a historic, though little-known, march from Boston to the spot in Nova Scotia over which we were now gazing. Today that distance is almost a thousand miles, but at that time, with no highways cutting through mountains and leaping over rivers, the distance for people on foot must have been at least a third greater. Many died and were buried by the wayside. Those who survived and reached this point were the forefathers of the people among whom we were now to live and work.

Bright and early the next morning, while we were still having breakfast, I got my first call. Our telephone had not been installed as yet, and the message was brought by a little girl who lived two doors away from us. She said that a man named Arno à Pierre wanted me *"aussitôt possible."*

I asked her who Arno à Pierre might be, and where he lived. To the second question she gave me a ready answer. He lived four miles away on the Chemin du Roi—the main highway in this area was always referred to as being the property of King George—in a house that was being newly painted and therefore would be about half-white and half-gray. But she had no answer to the first question. The man was simply Arno à Pierre, and she knew him well because he often came to her father's house, but, as far as she was concerned, he had no other name.

The use of Christian instead of surnames was, as I came to learn, a general custom here. It could hardly have been otherwise. Some ten thousand people, spread over the thirty-mile strip of seashore in this colony, shared about a dozen surnames. There were hundreds upon hundreds of Comeaus, Saulniers, Melansons, Belliveaus, Thibaults and Gaudets. To make matters worse, the number of Christian or first names was limited. There were dozens of Emil Comeaus, of Phillip Saulniers and Jean Gaudets. Nicknames were not, for some reason, very much in favor and therefore an individual would be identified, not only by his own name, but that of his father and often of his grandfather as well. For example Jean à Louis—John, the son of Louis—or Emil à Louis à Pierre. Married women were known by their husbands' first names, as Mathilde à

Louis, or Cecile à Charles. This in a way had a whole-some sound. Think of saying "John's Emily," or "Jim-my's Alice"!

All this I came to understand later. At the moment, however, I was concerned with Arno à Pierre, whatever his surname might be, and I decided to set off at once. I found the place without any trouble and was met at the door by Arno himself—a big, powerful, dignified-looking man. We exchanged a few words and then, to my surprise, instead of taking me into the house he led me over towards the barn.

He explained that one of his oxen had been gored dur-ing the night by another ox and that it had a bad wound in its shoulder. I was somewhat taken aback. My first patient an ox! I couldn't believe it for a moment. But there he was—fourteen hundred pounds of him, gazing at me sadly with big brown eyes. As I looked at the long shiny horns with brass tips, the thick brown and white hide, and the short muscular legs, my mind flashed back to a book I had once read by a famous London physician in which he told of cases involving the Duchess of X or the Count di Y. I remembered, too, a Dr. Kildare picture I had seen in which the patient was a terrific blond beauty. Suddenly I resolved that my patient would get just as good treatment as any Duchess, Count or movie actress.

Animals are very valuable to farmers and besides I like them, so my pride was not too sadly hurt at being asked to treat an ox. The wound was a jagged tear about six-inches long and an inch deep, which must be cleaned, the edges trimmed with scissors, sulfa powder put in and fi-nally closed with a dozen or more sutures. I wondered if the ox would like this attention and what he would do if he did not like it. I saw from the expression on his face that he was a pretty smart animal but that he would not take kindly to this sort of treatment. At that time there were no drugs readily available that could be given intravenously to a large animal like this to put him to sleep. Ether was a possibility but it would take gallons and it might result in his developing pneumonia. Then I remembered that Moise had shown me, in his blacksmith shop, a device he used for shoeing oxen—a large canvas sling that could be placed under the belly of the creature and a cranelike device for raising it off the floor. With his legs in the air, the ox was pretty helpless. I told Arno what I had in mind and he agreed to take the patient to Moise's shop in a truck.

Soon the huge sad-eyed brute was dangling comfortably with his hooves about a foot off the floor. We tied his legs together with a rope and we tied another rope to his horns and secured it to a beam in the ceiling. Now our patient would have to submit to the treatment whether he liked it or not. I went to work and, in the course of a half hour or so, got a good repair job done. Moise and Arno were very much impressed and told everyone I was a good ox doctor.

There was no veterinarian in the district and in the course of time I was to treat not only oxen, but foxes—these animals loved to chew each other's legs off—dogs, and even a few pigs. Once I did a hernia operation on an eight-inch-long pig. Unfortunately he developed pneumonia following the ether anaesthetic and died. I did not brag about these cases to my colleagues but I was not ashamed of them. Better doctors than I have been proud to treat these humble patients. Axel Munthe tells of some of his animal cases in the *Story of San Michele* and there was a man called Francis of Assisi who did the same thing, and look how great he became.

My first day in practice at Little Brook had begun curiously, but it was not over by any means. By ten o'clock my huge patient had been lowered to the floor and was on his way home, this time under his own power and at the rate of about one mile per hour. I was on my way to a bath—very thorough and prolonged—and breakfast.

I had barely finished my coffee when there was a gentle knock at the front door. A very frail old lady came in. She was dressed entirely in heavy black—in this neighborhood all old ladies dressed in black—and her face bore a thousand wrinkles but her eyes were bright and alert.

"You are the new doctor," she began, "Do you speak French?"

I replied in that language that I did speak French fairly well.

"Wonderful!" she said, and then continued to talk in English. "It is so nice to have a doctor who can speak French. One feels so much good if one can talk in one's own language. It is so much wonderful."

I don't know why, but I was to hear this speech a dozen times a day by people who insisted in speaking to me in English, however broken or imperfect. Perhaps it was because I came from the outside and they were skeptical about my really properly understanding them, but more likely they considered my French worse than their English. After all, the language they spoke was that which was spoken in France long before the French Revolution while Englishmen were still using the language of Shakespeare and could understand sentences like, "Art thou good at these kickshaws, Knight?"

My old lady told me that she had high blood pressure and that she had been obliged to "doctor for it" for a great many years. Also, that her husband was cranky and her son's wife was not all that she ought to be and that she had half a mind to put the younger people out of the house and let them look after themselves, only then there would be no one to milk the cows. All this worry, she said, certainly did not make her blood pressure any better and she needed medicine.

I took two of our kitchen chairs into the bare room which I had decided was to be my consulting room, and examined her. Her blood pressure was a hundred and eighty systolic and ninety diastolic. This is not an alarming blood pressure for an elderly woman. Women will go on for many years with a pressure much higher than this and finally, in advanced old age, die of some other condition. Still it should be treated.

It is not true to say that there is no effective treatment for hypertension. Even at that time there was much that could be done; today there is more. Why is it that hypertension is more serious in men than it is in women? Why do men have coronary disease so much more often than women? These are questions that will be answered someday, but nobody knows yet, despite all the theories that have been advanced.

I could not do a very thorough examination on the old lady because I had no equipment set up as yet. I explained this and told her that she was to return at a later date. I gave her a mild sedative—elixir of triple bromides —to take in the meantime, but as it happened her niece called me within a few days with the startling information that the old lady had gone out of her mind and would have to be sent to an institution for the care of the insane.

When I arrived at the home I found my patient was talking incoherently. She had delusions of persecution. She thought the end of the world was at hand and that the devil was making ready to claim her as his own. Her niece was in league with the devil and was conspiring to turn her over into his clutches. There was no doubt about it, the poor old woman was insane. Several neighbors were in the room and were trying to keep her from tearing the bed and her clothing to pieces.

I wondered what had brought this on. It is an unusual thing for an old person who has been normal all through life to develop this form of insanity. There seemed to be no doubt but that she would have to be committed and yet I hesitated to do so. It occurred to me that if I were to give her a good sedative and get her to sleep, we might at least be able to postpone the decision for a few days. Then I suddenly remembered that I had already given her a bottle of the elixir of three bromides. I asked the young woman if her aunt had been taking it.

"Oh, yes," she aswered, "she has been taking all her medicines."

"What do you mean by *all?* I gave her only one kind of medicine."

"But the other doctor gave her medicine, too."

"Please bring me the bottles," I said. She went into the kitchen and returned with three bottles. One was the bottle I had given her, another was the one given her by this other doctor and the third was a well-known patent medicine which is sold over the counter almost all over the world. A very brief investigation was enough to show that all three contained sodium bromide. I did some mental arithmetic. My patient was taking twenty-five grains of bromide salts three times a day!

Most people, if they take excessive doses of bromides for a period of time, are made aware of the fact in one of two ways. Either an ugly rash develops all over the body, which may cause them to seek medical advice, or they develop a general sluggishness of mind and body accompanied by a thickness of speech similar to the condition of alcoholic intoxication. In the exceptional case, however, the patient becomes irrational and can readily be judged insane. This is more likely to occur if the intake of common salt in the diet is low. I have since learned that many mental institutions make the testing of the blood for bromides a routine on admission. Who knows how many people have in the past been judged insane and committed to institutions because of this drug which is so widely used and has been popular for so many years! Certainly there must be hundreds, and perhaps thousands of people to whom this has happened.

I gave the old lady sixty grains of ordinary table salt three times a day, and stopped all the drugs. In a week she showed great improvement and in two weeks she was perfectly normal again. It taught me to be exceedingly careful when prescribing drugs to give my patients full and proper instructions.

My first day's practice in Little Brook went smoothly enough, after the ox was fixed up and the old lady sent home in all innocence to over-imbibe sodium bromide, and whenever I had a free moment I helped Sally unpack and organize our new home. We never could work long, however, without interruptions. A man came in complaining of a chronic cough; another man had an infected finger; a baby needed a new formula; a small boy had a rash. Then there was a lull and I was on a stepladder putting dishes away when I heard a car stop at the door and the sound of hurried footsteps.

"You the new doctor?" a man asked when I met him at the door.

"Yes," I said.

"Then please come quick to my house," he said, "we have a woman"—I knew he meant a midwife—"but something is going wrong. Please come right away!"

But when we arrived at his home, which was not more than half a mile away, we found a most happy situation instead of the scene of trouble which I had expected. Twin babies had been born in the few minutes the husband had been away. They lay in the bed still attached to their mother by the umbilical cords. The mother lay back exhausted, but happy and smiling. There was nothing for me to do except tie and cut the cords and express the afterbirth with a little pressure on the abdomen. I also put drops of silver nitrate solution in the babies' eyes and gave the mother an injection of Pituitrin as a protection against hemorrhage. When I had finished I stood back and looked at her.

She was almost middle aged, her features were coarse, rough and irregular, and obviously she was used to the heavy work of house and farm. But I thought she was beautiful. I don't know why it is that a woman who has just had a baby always looks beautiful. Dignity and an inner happiness radiate from her. If you have seen a glamorous movie actress on the screen, dressed and painted to look her most alluring, you still have not seen the ultimate in the beauty of woman. I have a personal theory about it. It seems to me that any woman who has gone through the travail has expiated for all of her past, no matter what that may be, and that she wears the stamp of God on her brow. There cannot be present "a multitude of the heavenly host," but I am sure that even to the lowest and most sinful woman on earth, God sends at least one small angel.

Obstetrics is, in general, satisfactory kind of work and most doctors realize this although they may complain about the hours and the getting up at night. For one thing, it is an art which today has been brought pretty close to perfection. The number of obstetrical procedures is limited. If he has the necessary good judgment and will exercise care, the doctor in Silver Creek, Arizona, can do absolutely anything that the Park Avenue specialist can do. For another thing, after a case is over, the patient is happy, the relatives are happy and everything is smiles and flowers. In these days tragedy very seldom appears.

When I had finished and was ready to leave, the man asked me what was the charge. I did not know what to say. I had done practically nothing—certainly not anything requiring any skill—and I had spent only about ten minutes in the house. I told him I would charge him ten dollars. He paid me at once and I went home.

This case had a curious and comic aftermath. For the next month or two I had any number of women and husbands come to me and ask if I did confinement cases for five dollars. They said they had heard I had charged ten dollars for two babies so they thought I should do an ordinary one-baby confinement for five dollars. I explained over and over that the regular charge for a case was twenty dollars, the prevailing fee for an obstetrical case in the area. I used to think ruefully of the hundred and five hundred dollar fees which some of my city friends charged. I have heard too of the thousand and five thousand dollar fees collected by some doctors in certain large cities. I suppose they use solid gold forceps and deliver only super-babies.

At about ten o'clock that night, Sally and I reviewed the events of the day. We had arrived in our new location at four o'clock the day before and we had already earned and *taken in* the sum of thirty-eight dollars. This was the largest sum of money that we had yet received for one day's work.

Chapter Twelve

STRANGE as it might seem, money continued to come in in fairly worth-while amounts and, as it came in, we sent it out again, as fast as the mail trains could carry it, to Montreal, Toronto and two or three other places. It was like pouring water into sand, so quickly did it disappear, but we knew that even sand can finally become saturated and we kept it up in great hope. We were very careful and determined not to buy anything we did not absolutely need until the day when we could afford it.

One of the things we lacked most was furniture. For chairs we had only the plain, straight-backed, hardwood kind that you could get at that time for a dollar apiece. A log or a rock is luxurious by comparison. The log has bark which cushions it at least slightly, and you can often find a rock that is shaped to fit. But we put up with those chairs for more than four months. Then at Christmas time we got a gift from Sally's people that was above rubies. It was a real chair—one with padding and cloth to cover it. We took turns sitting in it just for the sheer fun of sitting—a half hour on and a half hour off.

But even before we had that luxurious chair to offer an honored guest, our Little Brook friends were willing to spend evenings with us; they understood that fine furniture is not an absolutely essential ingredient for a successful party.

Hilarion, the policeman, was one of my early friends in Little Brook. His duties as defender of the peace took up only a small part of his time so he also was tax collector, mail-driver, farmer and meatman. It was in his capacity as meatman that we first became acquainted with him. He used to come to the door every morning, driving a small covered truck laden with meat. His prices were reasonable—fifteen cents a pound for round steak, eighteen for T-bone, twenty for tenderloin, and ten for stew beef. Liver was free—something for the cat. We had no cat, because Ronnie was allergic to the fur, but Hilarion kindly chose to ignore this fact and threw in a pound or two of liver with our other purchases. And two dozen miles away, outside the invisible boundaries of this colony, people were buying bologna at thirty-five cents a pound, and hamburg at forty cents!

Hilarion's family was an interesting one. His wife, Mathilda, had almost as many diverse occupations as her husband. In addition to her household duties, she hooked rugs, knitted socks and sold fire insurance. She also collected ox tallow, a by-product of her husband's business, and sold it to the shipyard for use in lubricating the skids on which wooden vessels were launched.

Mathilda's father lived with them—a man of about ninety, thin, ascetic and vigorous, as alert in all his faculties as any man of thirty. He was a scholar, and real scholars never grow old, at least not in the sense that other people do. In his youth he had been a schoolteacher, then a sailor, then a schoolteacher again, and finally postmaster in a neighboring village from which position he had retired only ten years before. He could talk with authority about the Rothliegende of Chemnitz, the cathedrals of Europe, or American foreign policy. But his special hobby was the history of Acadia. On this subject he was always ready to talk, and I—after we had become acquainted following a battle with streptococcus—was always ready to listen. He had a small museum in his living room—a dozen or so articles lying on a mantelpiece—and one day he showed me an instrument used by the early Acadians for extracting teeth. It was a very simple but effective device consisting of a short iron rod with a handle at one end and a swinging hook at the other. It worked after the principle of the peavey used by lumberjacks for handling logs; the more you turned the handle the tighter became the grip on the tooth. If Evangeline ever had a toothache, doubtless she was acquainted with this instrument.

Hilarion himself seemed to belong to another race than his father-in-law. He was a big man, red-faced and fat, as most butchers are, and at the same time strong-jawed and muscular as a policeman should be. His police work was not very arduous. Although he was responsible for a territory some thirty miles wide inhabited by about ten thousand people, he was seldom obliged to don his official uniform. Probably for three hundred and sixty-three days a year it lay in mothballs in a trunk.

Not that the place was free of crime. On the contrary it was seething with it. During the winter, for example, it was the duty of every able-bodied man—no matter who he might be—to turn out and shovel snow. If anyone defaulted he was hailed before the municipal court and, if found guilty, forced to pay a fine or go to jail. Every winter there were sure to be at least one or two defaulters, and it was the duty of Hilarion to arrest the criminals. Occasionally there were even more serious crimes than this. I remember hearing on one occasion that someone had broken into the spruce gum factory and stolen a pailful of spruce gum.

It was a surprise to learn that there were at least a half-dozen factories in the area—a shoe factory, a cosmetic factory and an overall factory, to mention only a few. Strangely enough, none of these was visible to the naked eye, until you knew about it. A typical manufacturing plant, exteriorly, was an ordinary house, painted white, with three gables, a flower garden in front, and children swinging on a gate. Nothing at all to indicate that inside five or six people, including the owner, his wife and his daughter, were busily at work turning out manufactured goods.

The output of a plant like this could not be very great, yet Melanson's Spruce Gum—an excellent product—is known in every town in eastern Canada. It is not as popular as Wrigley's Spearmint, perhaps, but it is still in demand by a great many people who like the smell of spruce forests better than that of mint. Comeau's shoes are as good, in quality of material and in honest workmanship, as the best and most expensive in the world. Yet very few people outside of Nova Scotia have ever heard of them. They are not advertised—and for a very good reason. The people who make them are satisfied with their small plant. They earn a good living. They are not interested in owning a sixteen-acre mass of brick and glass and turning out a Niagara of shoes. Let the people in Montreal and Toronto and the United States have the worry of running their huge factories! You don't often have strikes in a place where you, your wife, your son, and three or four of your next-door neighbors are the employees.

These people were independent of stores for most of the things needed every day. Each family had quantities of home-canned foods of all kinds. They grew their own vegetables and preserved them. They canned deer meat— deer was plentiful—chicken, pork and beef. They preserved eggs in water glass. They dug clams—huge ones as big as saucers—and canned them. They made cider—wonderful stuff—in order to save the government the trouble of printing excise tax stamps. They canned lobsters. After every big storm, you could go down to the beach and find quantities of small lobsters stranded between the rocks. It was easier than picking strawberries. Butter was preserved by adding plenty of salt to it. Every family had food stored away on shelves in the cellar for a year or two ahead. As for fuel, he was a poor farmer who did not have a two-year supply stored away. And because almost everyone owned his own home there was no worry about rent. In other words, they had security.

Seeing the way in which the people lived so well and so comfortably with a minimum outlay of money gave us the idea that we might well profit by their example. We decided to adopt some of their ways. Sally and I would make plans in the evenings when Ronnie had gone to bed, and sometimes we would open a bottle of cider, which we got from one of our friends, and when we did this we found that we could think much more clearly and make plans that were very, very good. We decided to start canning and preserving vegetables and fruit for ourselves. Also we would plant a garden, so that the vegetables would cost us absolutely nothing; and raise a pig and a dozen or two chickens. The pig and the hens could be fed with leftovers from the table, so that we would have, when fall came, vegetables, pork, poultry and eggs for the family at almost no cost at all.

But while we were still planning winter swept down with an abruptness that was frightening. One evening the ground was bare and the next morning we woke up to find it covered with almost two feet of snow. Then the wind came up and made the snow move and shift almost like the surface of the sea and, increasing in violence, whipped it into the air so that an object was not visible ten feet away.

That day we found out that our house, new though it was, was not meant for weather like this. The wind seemed to enter in a hundred places. The hinges and knobs of the doors were covered with frost on the inside even with a roaring fire going in our two stoves. Frost showed on the plaster just above the baseboards. Upstairs in a bedroom, water froze solid in a glass that stood on a table beside the bed, and metal doorknobs of bedroom doors were painful to touch. Near the stoves you could be warm; but only one side of you at a time.

Looking out through the window I could see drifts of snow four and six feet high on the road directly in front of the house. "I hope the telephone lines are down," I said to myself, feeling guilty at the same time. During storms people who are just a little bit sick call the doctor because they are frightened. But nobody would walk for a doctor in this storm even though they might expect me to walk to them.

It was cold near the window and I had started to turn away when I caught sight of the figure of a tall thin man who was having a struggle to reach the door. I went to meet him. When I opened the door, the blast of cold air that came in sent newspapers flying and picked a calendar from the wall. I caught the man by the sleeve, hauled him in and pushed the door shut.

He was a man I knew well. George Melanson was seventy-two years old, quite deaf, and lived about two miles down the road. How a man of his age had been able to struggle so far through this snow and storm was a mystery, but as soon as he had warmed himself at the kitchen stove and taken the hot tea which Sally had given him he explained that he had left home two hours earlier, before the wind had come up to full force and he had been only three or four hundred yards away from the house when the storm struck. It had taken him nearly an hour to cover that short distance. He had come to get medicine for a cold, he said! But I knew the real reason. A widower, he lived alone and he was lonely. He was a bit slow in thinking and he had misjudged the weather. Perhaps he had started out to go to the store, and finding it closed, had invented this excuse to come and see me.

It had never occurred to me that George knew any language but French. He had always spoken to me in that language and I had assumed that like so many of the old people in the area, he knew no English. When he was sitting by the fire and having his cup of tea, I introduced him to Sally. Now Sally knew he was deaf, because she had heard me talking to him, and when she shook hands with him and said, "How do you do, Mr. Melanson," she spoke in a normal low voice thinking that as he knew no English it made no difference whether he heard her or not. Then to the surprise of both of us he answered in English, clearly and well, "How do you do, Madam." But the accent in which he spoke was not French but definitely and unmistakably the accent of the Lowland Scot! I said, "I didn't know you could speak English, George."

"And why not," he said, "I was born in Aberdeen. And," he went on, "you don't need to talk so loud, Doctor. Someway I can hear much better this morning. Perhaps it is the storm or something."

It was not the storm, as I guessed at the moment and ascertained later, that had brought about the change. There is a difference in deafness. Here the mechanism of the ear was perfect, but the portion of the brain which received the impulses from the ear was impaired. I had, of course, long been familiar with this phenomenon of physiology—but that he should hear one language and not another was more amazing to me. Was there one spot in the brain to receive the French language and another for the English language? I did not think this could be the explanation.

Here was another peep into the mysterious complexity of the human brain. I think the patterns of speech recognition left on the little brain cells when the brain was that of a child were printed deep. The impressions that came later were more lightly printed on top of these. When old age takes up the eraser and begins to go over the blackboard of the human mind, its strokes are gentle at first. It passes lightly and only the lighter markings are obliterated, and then only in part. Later the strokes are more heavy. The Schoolmaster had said, "The Lesson is over!" This is the only way I can express it because it is the only way I can think of it. To me it is rather beautiful to think that as we get into our declining years one part of us becomes restored—not in its vitality of course, but in its simplicity—to what it was when we first, with so-wide eyes, greeted the world.

All day the wind howled and the four of us, Sally, old George, Ronnie and I, huddled around the kitchen stove. The teapot was going all the time. Sometime during the midafternoon, old George after a long period of smoking his pipe in silence, said, with no preamble or explanation, "I knew Jerome."

"I beg your pardon?" said Sally.

"I knew Jerome very well. I was at his funeral. He was a queer man."

Sally had never heard of Jerome, but I had, and of all the mysteries that have ever been associated with the sea, the case of Jerome is one of the most weird and fascinating.

"Sally doesn't know anything about Jerome, George," I said. "Suppose you tell it to her from the beginning."

At this he was pleased; it was a story he loved and he told it well.

"Well, Madam," he began, "it all happened a long time ago and it began right here—" he pointed out our front window. I looked at the window. The snow, driven by the fury of the wind, hissed against the glass like fine hard sand. Next to a fire in an open grate there is nothing better to watch while listening to a story.

One evening, in the spring of the year 1872, the residents along this shore saw a strange ship coming up the bay. At first they had not paid much attention to it because many sailing vessels used to go up and down the bay at that time. But when she came to anchor about two miles offshore, and showed no colors, as all respectable ships used to do, and when there was no sign of a boat putting in for shore, people began to get curious. But it was late in the evening and by the time somebody became sufficiently curious to get out a glass, it was too dark to see much. They could not make out her name or any special markings about her, but they could see that she was a good-sized ship, that she carried double topsails and topgallant sails, and gaff sails on fore- and mainmasts. The latter sails, I am told, were not common rigging at the time. During the night she showed no lights and at daybreak she had disappeared, apparently having slipped away in the dark.

In the morning a man named Albright, a fisherman who lived in Sandy Cove just across from Little Brook, was walking along the shore towards the spot where his boat was pulled up on the beach when all of a sudden his attention was arrested by a shocking sight. A man was lying there on the sand, terribly mutilated—both of his legs were cut off above the knees and the raw stumps were showing. When Albright had recovered his wits he turned and ran for help. Three or four of his neighbors hurried back with him and together they carried the unconscious man to the nearest house, which belonged to some people by the name of Morton. There they put him to bed and sent for a doctor and the sheriff.

When the doctor arrived and had examined the stumps, he stated that he believed, judging from the appearance of the raw muscle and bone, that the amputations had been done with an axe and not more than a few hours previously. There was a piece of rope tied tightly around each leg a few inches above the line of amputation, and he believed these tourniquets had been applied before the deed was done because the bleeding, while severe, had not been extreme. The man was unconscious due to shock and, to the surprise of everyone, the doctor gave it as his opinion that he would recover.

Detectives came from Yarmouth and from Halifax when the news got around, and asked questions. But all the information they could get was about the ship that had come and gone during the night. Nobody had heard any noises. No one had information to give, so they waited anxiously for the man to come back to consciousness, when he could tell them what had happened. He was a very young man. Some said they thought he was only about nineteen or twenty years old. They said he was handsome in appearance, that he looked like a man of education and refinement, and that the quality and cut of his clothes were such as are commonly associated with wealth and social position. His hands too looked as if he had never done any work in his life.

The police and various other people who came from the city waited around for days to hear what the mystery man would say when he regained strength. What fantastic tale of horror would he have to tell? The Morton house in the obscure village of Sandy Cove became the center of nation-wide interest as the news spread.

A day came when the stranger finally appeared to have recovered. The fever which had held him since the time he was found on the beach had subsided and the light of intelligent awareness came into his eyes. But now the mystery, instead of being solved, became even deeper and more sinister. The man refused to say anything at all. He refused to answer questions; even to speak. There was great consternation and much speculation when day after day passed and they could get no word out of him. Many theories were advanced. Some said he must be a deaf-mute—but even a deaf-mute can make signs, write or communicate with others in some way. This man did nothing of the kind. Then it was thought that he had lost his mind or had amnesia. But one day Mrs. Morton, his hostess, surprised him talking to one of her very small children. He stopped as soon as she appeared. The child was questioned but he was too young to be able to give any account of what the man had said. All they could get was a word that sounded like "Jerome" and thereafter the man was given that name.

When the hacked remnants of his legs had healed over and he was able to dress, it was naturally thought that the man would make some move to go back to the unknown place from which he had come. Elaborate plans were made to follow him in case he had made plans with some confidant to depart in secret. But nothing happened. It appeared that he intended to remain where he was.

Time went by and general interest in the mystery gradually faded. For several years, however, people continued to come from many parts of the world to visit Sandy Cove—people in search of missing relatives for the most part. He received them all patiently but would not speak a word. They could find out nothing about him. They could not even tell from what country he had come.

After a few years a man in the village of St. Alphonse about eight or nine miles from Little Brook took Jerome to live with him. This man's name was Jan Nicola. When Jan died, a family of Comeaus took Jerome, and with this family he lived for nearly forty years. He died in April, 1912, a few days after the *Titanic* disaster, and was buried in the cemetery at Meteghan, the next settlement to Little Brook and about five miles away.

This is the story that old George told us, with of course, many interruptions and pauses. Later I looked up the newspaper accounts, but they gave no new information. There was perhaps one thing which could be called a clue. It seems that years after he was found, a son of the Comeaus with whom Jerome was staying was visiting in New York and, in some way, some newspaper reporters found him out and reviewed the case in their papers. Soon after this, a strange woman called on Comeau at his hotel and told him that she thought the mystery man might be her brother. She said she came from Mobile, Alabama, and asked him to deliver a letter to Jerome. And here again was another frustrating mystery. The envelope was sealed but it bore no name. It was, in due course, delivered to Jerome, and he was seen to read it. But to the great disappointment of the expectant family, he showed no reaction. Almost immediately afterward he destroyed the letter by tossing it into the open fire.

There must be someone in the world who could furnish at least a clue to the solution of this mystery. The ship must have had a fairly large crew. Did they all keep as silent as Jerome until they went to their graves? Surely some one of them must have told somebody at some time. Could it be that somewhere today in the city of Mobile there is a house with an attic, and in that attic a trunk, and in the trunk some old papers that would furnish an answer? Perhaps . . .

Many theories have been advanced but I do not believe any of them has been thoroughly investigated. A rather fantastic one connects Jerome with the Bonaparte family and someone, I do not know who, has speculated that Jerome was selected to be the victim of a terrible revenge on the family in general. No mention is made of who the avengers might be. The victim must have known French because he appears to have spoken a few words to a four-year-old child who knew no other language, and his name was, or may have been, Jerome. Who can say that it is not true and that a blood relative of the great Napoleon does not lie in the little cemetery at Metaghan in Nova Scotia? Many believe that Jan Nicola knew the answer to the mystery. Jan, incidentally, was a Corsican!

Old George stayed with us all that day and part of the next before he could go home. He said he had never seen such a storm or such a winter.

I thoroughly agreed with him and hoped I would never

see another like it. Almost every day my little Austin got stuck in the snow, but each time there was a pair of oxen near by to pull me out. There was a diphtheria scare that year and every time a child as much as cut a tooth, I got a call.

At last winter withdrew, reluctantly, and spring came, and then for about a month and a half, almost every ox in the county had a turn at pulling me out of the mud.

As the mud began to dry up, we started in on our project for taking a leaf from the simple lives of our neighbors. I got a farmer to come over with his oxen to plow and harrow a piece of land for the garden. He wanted to do a little patch only, about twenty by thirty feet, but I told him I wanted a proper garden. He looked at me and shook his head but he got the land ready—about half an acre. When I started in to plant and then to weed, with Sally helping me, and when our backs were nearly broken, I decided that the farmer had been right after all. We ended by planting about one quarter of the ground he had prepared for us—more than enough as the event proved.

The pig was about a foot long when we got him, pink and white and clean—a beautiful little animal. We took to him and he took to us right away. We had a little house built for him and a nice little fenced-in yard so he could have plenty of room for exercise. This cost in all about twenty-two dollars and Sally said you could buy a lot of pork for twenty-two dollars, but I pointed out that the pen would last for years and could accommodate a new pig in it every year at no cost at all.

We built a place for the chickens, too. When they arrived they were only a day or two old and very cute. Ronnie would not hear of their being put out in the chicken coop. He insisted on their being kept in the house. As there was only a dozen of them and actually it was a little cold still, especially in the evenings, we agreed to let them stay in a box behind the stove for a few days. He played with them on the floor, carried them in his pockets and fed them cake. We had to check him when he started putting them on the table at breakfast time. One of them fell into a bowl of corn flakes and got wet with milk. In a few days the novelty wore off and the chickens went out where they belonged.

The first inkling we had that the pig might not be an entirely profitable venture was when we started to pay the feed bills. It turned out that the leftovers from the table for one day would not provide even a midmorning snack for him, and we seemed to be buying feed all the time. But, of course, we were pleased that he had such a good appetite.

The second shock we received was when he was about four months old. By this time he was about five feet long and huge all over. We no longer thought he was cute but we had developed an affection for him of a deeper and more enduring kind. One day one of our neighbors came over and we took him out to see the pig. He was a good practical farmer and I had always regarded him as a friendly and kindly man. He looked at our pig and said, "Certainly is quite a pig all right. You won't be short of pork this winter. You'll have to salt some of him down."

Of all the callous, brutal things to say! From that day on it was with a sinking heart that I brought out the three daily rations—double-rations now—to the pig. I hardly dared look him in the eye for fear he would read what was in my mind.

We never did eat any of him. We kept him until he was the biggest and fattest pig in the whole county and then we traded him to Hilarion for a hundred pounds of pork guaranteed to be part of somebody else's pig. In the end we figured out that we had lost only about thirty-two dollars on this venture.

With the chickens we did a little better. I don't think we actually got enough eggs to pay for the cost of their feed, but still we got quite a few. We never ate any of the chickens either, but for a different reason. Ronnie was big enough by now to go around seeking adventures and next to the pig, the hens were the big attraction. One day he found a bottle of nembutal capsules in my medical bag and decided to give them to his friends, the hens. The capsules were bright yellow and the hens were happy to find this new kind of corn. They ate them all up in no time. We found them all, later, staggering drunkenly around in their coop. They must have enjoyed it for a while, but unfortunately, Ronnie had given them all an overdose. They quietly and peacefully passed away in their sleep.

We did not try any more experiments with livestock. From then on, we decided, we would not seek to deprive the poor merchants of their living.

Summer here brought all the things that summer brings anywhere, but the first day of summer brought us something special. It was on the twenty-second day of June that I showed Sally a bunch of letters that I had ready for mailing.

"These are the last of them," I said. "I told you that five thousand dollars is only a hundred dollars fifty times!"

She was standing by the stove with a handkerchief tied on her head and she looked rather dusty and grimy. She did not say a word, and as I was going out to mail the letters I glanced back and I saw that she was crying.

That night we had a party. We invited everyone we

could round up on short notice. There was lots of cider and conversation and singing. It was a fine party and everybody went home happy. After it was over and we were alone, Sally and I had an extra glass of cider each, and we toasted each other. I suppose that was our biggest day since the day that Ronnie was born.

Most people, I think, are familiar with the feeling of lightness that comes when a long-standing debt is finally paid off. It is as if a cloud were lifted or a chronic nagging festering sore abruptly healed. To us the momentous day when the last of our bills was paid, brought more than relief, it also brought a resurgence of ambition. We could now clearly see the road leading to what I, at least, wanted most.

Chapter Thirteen

In SHAKESPEARE'S *Macbeth* there is a passage in which the guilty king, fearing for his life, encounters a witch and seeks a prophecy from her. She mixes a brew—the recipe is given in the play, and it's terrible—and then tells him, among other things, that he will never be defeated by "any man born of woman." In the course of time Macbeth is killed by Macduff, Thane of Fife, but the prophecy is "justified" by the fact that Macduff was not born of woman but was "from his mother's womb untimely ripped"—in other words he came into the world by Caesarean section. This seems like a cheap excuse for the witch, but it is good enough for the purposes of drama.

There are plenty of people in the world today who, like Macduff, entered it by way of a Caesarean operation. But there are very few persons living—perhaps not more than four or five among all the inhabitants of the globe—who have never come from a womb at all, although indeed, they had mothers; and fathers, too, for that matter.

One day a young woman came to my office and told me she was pregnant and that, although she was not due for another month, she was in labor. She said she was having pains every three or four minutes and that these were very severe. Premature labor is common, of course, so I did not think too much about it. I told her to go into the hospital at once. There was no hospital in the Little Brook area but we had an excellent one at Digby, not too many miles outside my territory. There, I said, I would determine whether or not the case was appreciably advanced. If it were not, I would give her morphine and progesterone in the hope of postponing the event until the due time. Premature babies are hard to look after and often die. If things were really advanced, however, we would let events take their course. In either case we would have her safely under observation.

She entered hospital and after the usual examination I told her that although pains had begun, they had not resulted in any progress. We would therefore give her morphine and see if we could carry her over. We gave her the drug, a quarter of a grain, and waited. An hour later I saw her again. She said the hypo had had no effect on her whatever. She was still having pains as badly as ever. In fact she said, they were worse. I watched her during a pain and I knew she was not exaggerating. Another examination revealed no evidence of progress. I ordered another quarter grain of morphine. A half hour passed and when I visited her again there was still no change. With each pain her face twisted in agony and I could see the perspiration break out on her forehead.

I was puzzled and waited a while, letting her suffer, because at the moment there was nothing else I could do short of giving her an anaesthetic, which would have been folly at that stage.

An hour went by with no lessening in the severity of the pains and still no progress whatever. Obviously, all was not well. I went back to her bedside and began to ask her a few questions. One of the things she told me, the significance of which did not strike me immediately, was that she had had an attack of abdominal pain when she was only about six weeks pregnant. Her doctor at the time thought it might be an attack of appendicitis of a mild nature. She had recovered in a few hours and therefore no operation or other procedure was done.

I watched her during the pains and I noticed that when they came she always put her hands instinctively to one particular area of the abdomen—the upper right area, over the liver. This was unusual to say the least, and I asked her about it. She said that most of the pain was localized in that one particular spot. It also struck me that the pains were unusually fleeting. I passed my finger over her abdomen very lightly just as one might run a finger over a piece of satin in order to feel the texture. To my surprise even with this extremely light pressure I could feel knees, elbows and a head, as clearly as if they had been just under the skin. It was then that it first struck me that I might have here the greatest of obstetrical rarities; an ectopic at or near term.

An ectopic pregnancy is one in which the baby is conceived, not in the womb, but in the Fallopian tube. This tube has an open end which lies near the ovary and through it the ovum, when it escapes from the ovary, floats down into the uterus or womb. To have conception take place in this tube is not, in itself, too uncommon. What usually happens, however, is that after four or five weeks, the fetus, growing too large for the tube, ruptures through it into the abdomen. This results in an internal hemorrhage which requires an emergency operation. Again it may pop out of the open end of the tube without rupturing it, and simply become lost in the abdominal cavity. In the extreme rare case, it may emerge from the open end of the tube and, implanting itself on the outside of the uterus or other organ, continue to grow. In thousands of years of medical history only a few score such cases have been recorded. It would be exaggerating only slightly to say that they occur about as frequently as meteorites fall through the roof and land on the dining room table while the family is at dinner. It was with rising excitement, therefore, that I set about exploring for signs to confirm or discount my suspicion.

Once the possibility occurred to me that this might be one of those rare cases, it was a fairly easy matter to establish the diagnosis; an X-ray confirmed it. I at once alerted the operating room staff and then went to the textbooks to see what I could learn. The story told by the books was not encouraging. Before the advent of modern surgery all such cases had resulted in deaths of both mother and child. After surgery had developed to the modern stage, quite a number of babies had been delivered living but most of the mothers were lost. The cause of death in all cases was the same; severe hemorrhage following attempts to remove the afterbirth. This organ is a network of large blood vessels, branching and rebranching into smaller and smaller ones and its purpose is to draw nourishment from the blood engorged tissues of the mother. In a case like this, it is intimately in contact with the large vessels of surrounding organs. When an attempt is made to separate the afterbirth blood flows like water from a tap. No method of blood transfusion could keep up with the loss. In recent years some surgeon had thought up the idea of leaving the organ exactly where he found it, taking a chance on the possible ill effects that might result. In this way, some lives had been saved. This was the procedure I decided to follow.

The operation itself was a simple matter. The patient was wheeled into the operating room and the anaesthetic begun. I had quite a gallery that day. Word of the interesting case had gone around the hospital and everybody who could do so came in to watch. There were three staff doctors, and ten or twelve graduate nurses in the operating room besides the anaesthetist, assisting surgeon and the operating room nurses. There is something stimulating about working in front of a gallery. I suppose anybody who likes his work also likes to have other people see it. Perhaps it is the childish instinct to "show off" which persists to some extent and which up to a point is not always a bad thing. A gallery is no distraction to a surgeon. After he has made the first incision he becomes completely oblivious of everything else.

One careful, light stroke of a scalpel and a little hairy head popped into view. I picked the little creature out with no difficulty except that it was necessary to pry the fingers loose from a portion of intestine on which he had taken a tight grip. It is an interesting fact that there was no membrane surrounding the baby, and no fluid. The membrane had been ruptured previously by the kicking infant and had retracted. The fluid had absorbed. When I delivered him I found that one foot was up under the liver. It was apparently the striking of this foot against the liver, when the baby kicked, that had caused all the pain; not contractions of the uterus. The cord was cut close to the afterbirth after being carefully double-tied, and the abdomen was closed.

The woman made an uneventful recovery, but I kept her in the hospital a little longer than usual. I saw her every month after that. Five months later, the afterbirth could still be felt through the abdominal wall as a firm mass the size of an orange. Seven months later it had diminished to the size of a walnut. In nine months it could not be felt at all. The mother is well and happy today.

If I am ever tempted to puff up with pride over the successful outcome of that ectopic pregnancy, all I have to do is remember another kind of case in which I proved the old saying that a little learning is a dangerous thing. The adage is especially applicable to a doctor who attempts to invade a branch of medicine in which he has had inadequate training. I had had about twelve lectures on psychiatry, in medical school, I had read a couple of books on psychoanalysis, and worked for a year in a mental institution; in short, I had just about enough knowledge to be very dangerous indeed.

There was an unmarried woman about thirty-five years old who used to come to me week after week with complaints of having sore stomach, dizzy spells, weak feelings and the whole list of things that you read about every day in the advertisements for somebody's new wonderful discovery which retails at your neighborhood drugstore for only sixty-nine cents a bottle. For years before I saw her she had been visiting other doctors. They had done everything that could be done in the way of using modern methods of diagnosis and had failed to find any physical cause for her trouble. When she first came to me I sent her to the hospital and put her through the same routine with the same result.

She lived with two aged aunts who were almost helpless and on whom she had to wait hand and foot. This had been going on for years and she was physically and mentally exhausted. She could not go out among people because she feared to leave the old ladies for more than an hour at a time. Other people of her own age, who might have been her friends, were discouraged from visiting her by the presence of the two good but dull old people who sat silently in their rocking chairs in the tiny kitchen. So she had gradually fallen into a solitary life of drudgery. As time went by she saw her youth slipping away and no prospect of release for years to come. She was a person without very much education and it was inevitable that she should come to translate her mental frustrations into symptoms of physical disease.

She did not tell me at once of her troubles at home. When she visited my office she simply talked about her stomach, the discomfort, the pain, her inability to eat anything, the value or lack of value of baking soda, and the question of whether or not she had an ulcer. Unfortunately, when I decided to apply some of my great psychiatric knowledge to the problem, I thought only in terms of curing her stomach complaints. Remembering my lectures in psychiatry and the plausible-sounding books I had read, I reasoned that if I could get this woman to understand the basic foundation of her illness, if I could get her to realize that her symptoms were manufactured in her subconscious to mask the great frustration hidden there, then she would be cured.

So the next time she came to me, I reviewed her life for her. I told her that she was desperately unhappy because of the unfortunate situation at home, that she had been robbed by cruel fate of the normal life which should have been hers. I went on in this vein for quite a long time and then I explained the workings of the subconscious mind and told her that all her symptoms were manufactured by this subconscious in order to cover up the real cause of her unhappiness. I got results. Weeping, she admitted that I was right and that she was the most unfortunate and unhappy woman in the world.

The next day I had a call from her neighbors. I went out to see her and found her in bed. She was too weak to get up, she said. She told me between sobs how grateful she was to me for having opened her eyes to the terrible truth. She told me she had given up the best years of her life and now she was through. There was nothing left for her except to die, and she felt that her departure from this world was not far off. Already, she said, she had a weak feeling around her heart, and her limbs felt funny.

Needless to say I was appalled at the damage I had done and did my best to rectify it. But it was no easy matter. My speech had made her sorry for herself, and now she referred no longer to her stomach but to her supposedly failing heart. She remained in bed for more than a year! Neighbors came over daily to do things for the three of them, the aged aunts and my patient. She called me on an average of once a week because she thought she was dying.

Luckily, after a year or so, I was able to get her to a doctor who really knew something about psychiatry, and he cured her. At least she got back on her feet, started to work again and to carry on as she had been doing before. The psychiatrist explained to me the approach I should have taken with her. This woman, he said, had a secret wish that both her old aunts would die so that she could be free. She was a good and religious person and she felt guilty about the wish; so guilty in fact that she would not admit the thought to her conscious mind. The treatment was to get her to bring out or admit that secret desire which she had been suppressing for so long, and show her that it was a perfectly natural feeling under the circumstances and that she need not feel guilty about it at all.

From that day on I was very careful not to meddle with psychiatry, except for the simple common-sense kind.

Doctors, like everyone who deals with people in crises, do of course have to make frequent use of their knowledge of human nature, and they had better have a pretty good stock of it on hand for the occasional emergencies when they are called upon to be heroes.

There is nothing more exciting than being a hero. I am sure that if one were to ask Rickenbacker or Admiral Byrd or somebody like that they would say the same thing. I don't know if my exploit in Little Brook on a certain September day puts me in the same class as these two men, but I am inclined to believe that it does. On thinking it over I'm not sure that, everything considered, my own adventure was not even greater than any of those of— but there; heroes should not make comparisons. One should not care about these things. But still I think the newspapers should be more fair in distributing their laurels.

About fifteen miles from the village there was a small hamlet—actually just about five or six houses and a store. I wish there had been a Western Union office there so the world would—but that is not important. One morning I got a call to go to this little village. They told me a man there had gone crazy and that they needed a doctor right away.

It was one of those fine bright crisp mornings just suitable for hero work. When I arrived I found some twenty-five or thirty people milling excitedly around a house but keeping at a safe distance from the front door which was open and which they were watching with great apprehension. As soon as I got out of the car they all came over to me and told me about it. Pierre à Willie had gone out of his mind, they told me, and was threatening to kill the first person who crossed the threshold of his door, with a long knife which he was whetting at that very moment. Also he had heard some of them talking about getting a doctor and he had specified that if any doctor dared to enter his house he would get very special treatment with the knife.

Was I frightened? Certainly not! It is true that due to the fact that I had eaten something for breakfast to which I was allergic—I think it must have been the orange juice —I was not feeling very well. My mouth was dry so that I could hardly talk, my throat was tight so that I could hardly breathe, my heart was pounding and I had a weak feeling both in my stomach and my knees, but this was due to the orange juice. Any person who has ever had an allergic reaction will recognize the symptoms at once. Certainly it never occurred to me to be afraid.

I knew Pierre very well. He was, or had been, a good average farmer, a big man, quite intelligent, but somewhat inclined to drink too much at times. I was sorry to learn that he had gone out of his mind. Now, mental patients in general can be handled fairly easily by one who knows how. They can be reasoned with as a rule. This may sound strange but it is true, as anyone with experience knows. Mentally defective people such as idiots, morons, etc., are in a class by themselves, of course. They can be very dangerous. But if a person is intelligent, even though his intelligence is temporarily scrambled, and if you can get within talking distance of him and know what to say, you can generally, if not always, handle him. I proposed to try to talk to Pierre—from a safe distance of course.

To my gratification the people tried to stop me. They said it was sure death, virtual suicide, to go near Pierre. If I were to go near the door and listen, I would hear him whetting the knife. Just the same I thought I would at least look in. I told them so. They again tried to dissuade me, but I thought I knew Pierre well enough at least to have a look.

When I approached the door, walking very slowly in case the allergy should get worse, one of the men offered to come in with me. Now this posed a problem. If I had a man with me and Pierre attacked him first, I should have to come to his aid, there would be a fight and somebody might get hurt. However, if I were to go in alone, and the poor demented man came after me, I could gracefully and rapidly retreat; it is no particular discredit to a man to retreat when he is full of orange juice. No, I announced, I would go in alone; I did not want to endanger any more lives than necessary. At this they looked at me in awe.

I held my medical bag in my left hand as I started towards the door. A bag like this makes a good shield. It is thick and heavy and I have often used it for protection when I have gone to lonely farmhouses guarded by big dogs—there are a number of dog-teeth marks on mine. I walked slowly towards the door. True enough, I could hear the sound of someone whetting a knife.

I took two or three careful steps inside and towards the room in which Pierre was waiting. Suddenly the whetting sound stopped. The door was slightly ajar. I craned my neck and through the opening I saw Pierre sitting at a table with the knife in his hand. He too was craning his neck to see who was coming. As soon as he saw me his tense grim attitude changed. He dropped the knife on the table, stood up and came forward to meet me and not with any threatening gesture. When I saw this I pushed into the room and held out my hand to him. He took it and broke out into sobs.

"I'm sick, Doctor," he said, "crazy sick. I've been drinking for a few days and not sleeping. I think I'm going crazy and everybody has been coming around the house and picking at me. I'm awful glad you came. Do something for me, Doctor."

"Sure, Pierre," I said, "I'll fix you up in no time. You sit over here for a minute. I'll examine your heart and then I'll give you something to fix you up. But first," I said, "let me get rid of this."

Now I did something which I still blush to recall, but which at the time I just couldn't help—the temptation was too strong. I picked up the knife by the blade, walked out to the front door and in the sight of all those eyes, threw it carelessly out on the grass. I didn't say anything. You know that casual, silent way heroes have of doing things!

When I started back in to Pierre they all moved in a body to follow me in, but I stopped them. I talked a few minutes to the patient and then I gave him an injection of two hundred milligrams of thiamine chloride. This is the ordinary B_1 that is so familiar. In large doses like this it is often a miracle drug for people with acute alcoholic insanity. Then I gave him a sedative. I called his wife in and a few of the neighbors, and told them what to do for Pierre. He would go to sleep, I told them, and awaken perfectly well. I also sent one of them to town with a prescription. When you give large doses of thiamine like this it is also necessary to give a counterbalancing preparation to insure against harmful effects.

Pierre got well just as I had predicted. To my disappointment Sally was not too much impressed when I told her about this adventure, even though I forgot to tell her about the peaceful way in which Pierre had put the knife down on the table. She knew me too well, and besides she has, in addition to her itchy palm faculty, a knack for mind reading. As soon as I had told her the story she said, "Hmn" and then went on to tell me in detail what had really happened. I have long since almost stopped trying to tell her lies. That is another lesson I have learned in practical psychology.

Chapter Fourteen

N O TOWN looks the same to a doctor as it does to other people. There are a lot of secret doors in it which he and no one else may enter, and herein lies much of the fascination which the practice of medicine has for those who devote their lives to it.

There was a little corner store not far from the village, into which I used to go once in a while to buy cigarettes. It was not a very bright or modern little shop. It had a number of showcases arranged to form three sides of a rectangle and containing pipes, cigar holders, cigars, a few nickel-plated watches of the dollar-fifty variety, one gold watch in a velvet case, a display of straight razors, etc. All of these objects were dusty and looked as if they had been there for a long time and were due to stay there indefi-

nitely. On one of the showcases there stood a stuffed
eagle, its feathers also dusty and colorless in keeping with
the general air of the shop. The back part of the store
was partitioned off from the front and served as living
quarters for the storekeeper and his wife.

Peter Barnett who owned the store was a tall, thin,
silent man who seemed to be preoccupied all the time and
not at all anxious to see customers. His wife Matilda was
a woman of about forty years of age. At first glance she
looked dull and drab, but I have a habit of giving people
more than a quick glance and it seemed to me there was
something different about her that was not obvious on
the surface. At least, looking back on it after these years,
I seem to remember that I saw something in her.

One evening after supper, Peter called me on the phone
and asked me to come and see his wife. He told me that
she had been sick for the last two days and that he thought
she was getting worse. I drove out to the little shop and
Peter steered me around the glass showcases into the back
section and into the bedroom. Mrs. Barnett was not very
ill, as I found after examining her. She had a sore throat
and was running a slight temperature. I prescribed something for her and told her to stay in bed and rest.

When I had finished with this part of the visit I did
not leave at once. They were people who had few friends
and were alone most of the time, and I thought I'd spend
a few minutes getting acquainted with them. That is another habit of mine. Among other things, I asked them
how long they had had the little store and where they had
come from originally, and here I struck an unexpected
reaction. People are generally only too anxious to talk
about themselves to an interested listener, but these two,
after a quick glance at each other, shut up like clams. I
did not press the point but changed the subject and in a

little while I left, but I admit I was curious to know more about them.

In the following weeks I kept going into the little store at intervals to buy cigarettes or matches just as I had done before, and one afternoon Matilda saw me and invited me to come into the back and have a cup of tea with her and Peter. She showed me into the living room, a pleasant, bright, homey place. Besides the usual furniture there was an old-fashioned player piano in a corner and the top of this was covered with books. There were also two sets of shelves in the room and these too were filled with books. Mrs. Barnett brought in tea and biscuits on a little table and we sat around and chatted for perhaps fifteen or twenty minutes.

A few days later they invited me in again. From that time on it came to be a pleasant little habit and hardly a week went by when I did not have tea with Peter and Matilda, but never in all these conversations did they mention their past history.

One day, however, after I had known them for about two months, our innocent teatime conversation suddenly took an unexpected and grim turn. After a little pause Matilda said, with a glance at her husband which showed me that this was prearranged between them, "You know, Doctor, Peter and I aren't going to live very much longer. We don't expect to be here in six months' time."

I laughed rather awkwardly and started to say something, but she interrupted.

"Never mind, Doctor, we're serious. We are not joking and we are not crazy, although you might think so. We are going to die within six months and we know it and we don't mind a bit!"

I must admit I was shocked. It is not often you find two people sharing the same delusion at one and the same time. Yet while she was telling me this, Peter was nodding agreement with her.

"Look here, my friends," I said, "this is nonsense and you know it. I don't believe for a minute that you can be serious. You two have been living too much alone. Your imaginations are playing tricks on you."

They smiled knowingly at each other. Then Peter said in a matter-of-fact way, "But it's perfectly true all the same, Doctor. We'd like to tell you how we know and all about it. How much time have you got?"

"Plenty of time," I said. I would not have left at this point if the Prime Minister of Canada had been in my waiting room.

"All right," said Peter, "I'll tell you the first part and then Matilda can finish it at the place where she comes in. Let's all have another cup of tea first." Matilda poured the tea and then Peter began.

He had hardly spoken two dozen words before I knew that what he was recounting was fact and not the product of imagination; I had heard it before, a long time ago and in a place many miles away.

About one hundred and fifty miles northeast of the city of Halifax, there is a small town called Antigonish. There is no other town within a radius of forty miles. The surrounding country is very thinly populated. Farms are scattered far apart, as if hiding from each other, and the people who live there, for the most part, lead a lonely quiet existence. At a point about twenty miles from Antigonish there is a place known as Caledonia Mills. It can hardly be called even a village because the houses are so dispersed, but one of the farmhouses has a sign on it saying "Caledonia Mills Post-Office," and therefore the place has a name.

At one point there are some lonely ruins on the side of

a hill. In the year 1922 instead of these ruins there was a small neat house there, painted white, and in this house lived three people, Alexander MacDonald, his wife Mary, and an adopted daughter called Mary Ellen. One cold morning in January, when the snow lay three feet thick on the ground isolating them from the outside world, these three people were gathered in the kitchen of the little house. Mrs. MacDonald was washing the breakfast dishes and Mary Ellen was helping her. Mr. MacDonald had just finished feeding the stock, and, having no other duties for the time because of the weather, was settling down for a comfortable morning in the warm kitchen.

Suddenly, all three were startled out of their morning peace by the smell of smoke—smoke that did not come from the stove. The house was on fire, and the smoke was coming from the next room. Alexander MacDonald picked up a pail of water and ran into the room. He saw no fire, but he saw smoke drifting down from upstairs. He took the steps three at a time and, in the room just above the kitchen, he found that the floor was burning in a small area near the chimney. It was a small fire and when he dashed water on it it went out immediately.

Relieved at the narrow escape from losing their home, none of them noticed that although the fire was near the chimney, it was not next to the chimney. When they were satisfied that the charred section of floor was completely cold they started downstairs, thankful that it was all over, and wondering a little how it had started. In the kitchen they sat down to talk about it when Mrs. MacDonald gave a cry of alarm.

In the living room through which they had just come, there was a little yellow flame rising from an old-fashioned couch. A pillow was burning. Alarmed and frightened they ran in. Alexander picked up the pillow by one cor-

ner, ran with it to the door and threw it out in the snow.
The two adults and the young girl looked at each other
in wonder. The place was full of smoke and they kept
peering nervously about them. Mrs. MacDonald decided
to pour some more tea and in a few minutes they settled
down again.

Some twenty minutes went by and then Alexander
jumped up quickly, almost upsetting the table. In a corner of the kitchen, just over the sink, a towel, an ordinary
towel which they used to dry their hands, was burning
brightly and flames were licking at the wall behind.
Trembling, he dashed over, flicked the towel into the sink
and poured water over it.

He was still gazing in fascination at the charred wet
cloth in the sink when there came another cry. He turned
quickly. His wife and Mary Ellen were staring through
the open door that led into the living room. There, on
the bare wall, about two feet above the couch, a patch
of wallpaper about six or eight inches in diameter was
afire.

MacDonald must have been a man of great self-posses-
sion. He immediately shouted to his wife and the girl to
run for help, and rushed to the new outbreak. He put
this fire out easily by slapping it with the wet towel which
he had taken with him from the sink.

The woman and the girl hastily threw on their coats
and ran out into the deep snow in which they floundered
up to their hips. When they were gone Alexander ran
back into the kitchen and glanced quickly into all the
corners. He was afraid to think. He was afraid to stop
and wonder how a patch of paper on the wall could burst
into flames with no source of heat at hand.

He ran upstairs; nothing there except the smoke from
the first fire. He came down again and kept marching

from room to room watching everywhere, turning his head quickly to look behind him every few minutes—afraid to look and yet afraid not to look. Every now and then he glanced out the window in the direction of the house of his nearest neighbors, the MacGillivrays. Five, ten, twenty minutes passed and there were no new fires. When a half hour had gone by he again looked out of the window and saw in the distance a little group of people coming. He was relieved, but he did not cease his vigil, and while he watched there were no new fires.

In a little while the relief party arrived. There were five or six of them, men and women. They talked excitedly and went around the house looking at the burned places, wondering, suggesting possible theories. But none of them spoke of the one theory which was uppermost in their minds.

Mrs. MacDonald made more tea and started to pass cups around when someone cried, "What's that?" There was a noise upstairs, a crackling noise. In a body they dashed up. A door was burning brightly—a small blaze, but bright, directly in the center of one of the panels. One of the men took off his macintosh and blotted the fire out as one would erase a blackboard. But the charred spot was not erased. They looked at it in wonder until someone shouted that there was smoke coming from another bedroom. There again they found a blaze—wallpaper again, a spot about nine or ten inches in diameter and directly over a bed. There was something especially ominous about the wallpaper blazes. Light a newspaper and hold it against a papered wall. You will scorch and blacken the paper but you will not set it afire unless you have such a blaze as will burn the house down. But the wallpaper was ablaze and in a small patch. They put out this fire, too.

There was a noise downstairs. More reinforcements had arrived. Somehow all the people in the valley had heard about what was going on and they kept coming in numbers. Within a few hours there were at least fifty people in the house. Every room in the house, upstairs and down, was filled with people. They were on the stairs and in the hallways, and still the fires continued. Every few minutes someone would cry out, "Here's another one." Cushions, pillows, bedspreads, books, clothing, parts of doors and other woodwork, would burst into flames. Sometimes, but not often, two blazes would be discovered simultaneously. All day this continued.

Night came and the watch was increased. To the surprise of people with fixed ideas concerning the association of weird events with the hours of darkness, the fires were much fewer in number. With the coming of the dawn, however, the events of the previous day started all over again.

In a short while the news spread by phone to the town of Antigonish, and soon people began to arrive from there by sleigh—newspaper people and police. From Antigonish the news flew on the wires to Halifax and editors in the offices of the Halifax *Herald* and the *Morning Chronicle* hurriedly got together crews of reporters and photographers and dispatched them by train to the scene of the strange occurrences. And they sent the news on the wires again to the faraway city of New York and from New York it sped to Detroit and Chicago and London and Los Angeles and all the great cities of the world. In Paris and London and in faraway Australia, husbands looked up from their papers and said to their wives, "Look what it says in the paper," and their wives listened and said, "Just think! Isn't that strange," and went on about their business. In small villages in Connecticut and New Hampshire, Ohio and Arizona, and in the Yukon territories and Alaska, people gathered around stoves in their village stores and began telling ghost stories again—stories that had gone out of fashion since electricity had come to chase away the shadows.

Days passed and in the little farmhouse in the remote little settlement the mysterious flames still broke out and were as quickly extinguished by the hundreds of volunteers who now took turns in watching every room and closet, every nook and cranny.

And now new things began to occur. Horses and cows were found turned about in their stalls or tethered to impossible places in the barn. There were reports of people being slapped by invisible hands or tripped by invisible obstacles.

Then abruptly, everything ceased. No fires, no mysterious tampering with the cattle—nothing! It was almost as if a sharp command had been given by some invisible Authority. People milled around for several days and then, one by one, they left to go about their business.

The newspapers however, were loath to see the end of the mysterious happenings which had fed their presses. They engaged Dr. Walter F. Prince, a scholar of high repute, to conduct an investigation.

Dr. Prince traveled to Halifax and from there to the scene of the weird occurrences. He took up residence in the now-deserted house in company with three other men, two detectives and one representative of the press. The four remained in the place for several days. They examined everything and questioned scores of witnesses.

In the end Dr. Prince issued a carefully worded statement to the press in which he guardedly admitted that no proper, natural explanation of the phenomena was to be found. He raised a question as to whether the adopted daughter Mary Ellen might not have been an agent in the case. She was known to have been a young person of less than average mentality. But it was argued that if she were responsible she would have had to have an ability greater than that of Harry Houdini, for it would have taxed the skill of the great magician himself to cause even one small blaze to break out spontaneously on a patch of wallpaper or in the center of a door panel, in front of a score of witnesses. There are chemicals by which such an effect can be produced—given time for proper stage setting—if one has a good knowledge of chemistry, skill in using the materials and a source of supply. It is not likely that Mary Ellen had any of these requirements.

Dr. Prince wrote a more detailed report for the *Journal of the American Society for Psychical Research*. This report is a cautiously scientific account of his investigations. He draws no careless conclusions. In the end he admits only that he can find no natural explanation to fit all the facts.

The MacDonald family never returned to their home. The little house was left deserted. There it stood for some time, until one night a sudden blaze illuminated the countryside. The house was enveloped in flames. I do not know if any attempt was made by the people on surrounding farms to put the fire out, or if they simply gazed at the blaze in wonder. At any rate, this time the mystery house burned to the ground.

While Peter had been telling me this long story—which I already knew well—Matilda Barnett had been sitting motionless in her chair facing me. I glanced at her from time to time and I thought she looked tense and nervous. One or twice she gestured as if she were about to interrupt her husband, but she restrained herself and remained silent. All during Peter's recital I had been wondering what conceivable connection there could be between this strange story and the queer delusion which the two of them had concerning their own future. Where did they come into the case? I felt that as soon as it came Matilda's turn to speak I'd know the answer, and when Peter had finished, I turned to her with great attention.

"Now," she began, "I know, Doctor, that you have been wondering what we have to do with all this. Well, I'll tell you. In the first place, Peter and I have not always lived here. We were born in Guysboro County, and when we got married we took up a farm a few miles on the Guysboro side of Glencove. Do you know where Glencove is?"

"Yes," I told her, "Glencove is only a few miles from Caledonia Mills."

"That's right. And we were living there in the winter of 1922 when these things happened. I remember it as if it were yesterday—all the excitement and everything. Well, there's one thing Peter left on purpose for me to tell you. You know on those days that all the fires were breaking out by themselves and all the neighbors were watching and putting them out, well, Peter and I were two of those neighbors. We saw everything and it was just as Peter told you. And we saw something that Peter didn't tell you. We saw something nobody else saw."

"Just a minute, Matilda," Peter interrupted. "What we saw was not in the MacDonald house. You must explain that to the doctor."

"That's right," said the woman, "it was after we got home that we saw it—the same night the fires stopped. Before we left the MacDonald house, I picked up something for a souvenir, and took it home. It was a piece of burned pillowcase, just a small piece about six inches long and six inches wide and one side was charred. And that night we saw it." She drew a deep breath. "We were in bed but we weren't asleep yet or, at least, Peter was asleep but I wasn't. I was facing towards the wall and my eyes were open looking towards the bureau although I couldn't see it because the room was dark. Then all of a sudden I saw a little glow in the dark, just over the bureau and it seemed to be around the little bit of pillowcase which I had put there, and I saw numbers made of fire and they said '*1939.*' "

She stopped, and after a moment Peter said, "I saw it too. She woke me up and I saw it, the number 1939 in glowing figures. I got up and lighted the lamp and then the numbers went away."

I sat back in disappointment and yet with relief. I knew scores of people in the Caledonia Mills area who "saw things" for years after that eventful January. In the state they must have been after coming from that house it would be an easy matter for Peter and Matilda to "see" the numerals 1939. It would almost have been more surprising if they had not seen anything. But their present queer delusion was another matter.

"And what has this got to do with the foolish idea that you are both going to die soon?" I asked.

Peter said, "It was plain that the year was to mean something for us. Something important. And, well, we just *know* that it means this is our year to die."

After that it was I who did most of the talking. I tried to explain to them that the events they had witnessed at the MacDonald house had worked on their imaginations and had resulted in their seeing things which were not present. I told them of the other people I knew who had imagined they saw things but who had not been carried away by their fancies. I told them a few simple little things that I had learned in the study of psychology. But they were not impressed. To everything I said, they would ask, "But why 1939, Doctor?"

The only answer I could think of was, "Why not 1939 as well as anything else?" I talked to them for a long time and finally I had to give up.

The next day I went back and again I argued and reasoned with them, but again with no result—I could make no impression on them whatever. They kept assuring me that they did not mind dying and that they were not afraid. I was getting nowhere. Finally, I said, as an afterthought, "By the way, to what religion do you belong?" They hesitated and then Peter answered, "We don't belong to any church, Doctor." There was a pause and then Matilda said, "We used to be Catholics, a long time ago."

That gave me an idea. I have often called on clergymen to help in odd cases. Sometimes they can do better than a psychiatrist. At different times I have called on ministers of every major denomination. Religion, no matter what particular form it takes, is not a force to be neglected.

I did not say anything to Peter and Matilda at the moment, but that night I called on Father Chapdelaine. He was a pious man who had plenty of common sense and a sense of humor as well. I told him as much of the story as I could and he agreed to visit the Barnetts. He went to see them the next day and almost every day afterward.

I continued to call in to see the Barnetts as I had done before, and gradually I could see a change come over them, and I knew Father Chapdelaine was getting in his work. One day I found Peter dusting off the eagle and trying to put its glass eye back in place. I helped him with the eye and then Matilda walked into the shop from the back. She looked different. Some of the strained look was gone from her face and she seemed younger. We chatted for a little while about events in the village and, for the first time, they seemed to be interested in what was going on. When I left that day I felt that they were on the way to being cured.

But I cannot let Father Chapdelaine take all the credit for the end result. One evening towards the end of the "cure" I went to visit Peter and Matilda after office hours and with me I brought, as a kind of treat, a quart of Teachers Highland Cream. I should explain that this Highland Cream is not anything like the cheap, no-good product that you buy from your milkman for only ninety cents a pint. It comes from Scotch cows which are fed exclusively on a special kind of heather, and in the dairy it goes through a secret decolorizing process that takes away the sickly, repulsive creamy-white color and leaves it a beautiful, lovely, crystal-clear transparent amber. We each had one or two tastes and we could feel the nourishing value of it right away. We talked for a while about good earthy things and then I remember that I sat down at the old player piano and very skillfully played two rolls —while Peter and Matilda sang.

And I think this marked the completion of their cure.

Chapter Fifteen

TWO years went by. During that time great events were taking place in distant corners of the globe—events which, world-shaking as they were, echoed only faintly in our sheltered retreat. For us life went on at a fairly steady tempo. I suppose I delivered two or three hundred babies in those two years, removed about the same number of appendices and other organs—as varied in nature as the stock in trade of a pawnshop—made a couple of thousand home visits and saw four or five thousand people in my office. Sally answered the telephone or the doorbell a quarter of a million times—her own estimate—did her housework and took time out to have a new baby. He was born in March and we called him John. Although we gave him only one name instead of four, as we had

done with Ronnie, we were as proud and happy as if we
had never seen a baby before.

Altogether it was an idyllic sort of life.

I suppose we didn't really appreciate Little Brook or
realize how remarkable a place it was until the day The
Letter came.

I remember the occasion well. It was a fine sunny afternoon in June. I had come home between calls to bring
Sally a piece of news which I thought would make her
very happy.

"Listen, dear," I said as I came in the door, "I have
something wonderful to tell you. You know the little new
house with the elm in front and the flagstone path leading
down to the water that you were saying you liked so much
last week? Well, it's for sale. And do you know what a
person could get it for? Only two thousand, five hundred
dollars."

She looked at me with a shrewd eye.

"Well," she said, in a voice that was flat and not a bit
excited, "what about it?"

I was surprised. I had expected her to jump for joy;
she had talked about that house so much.

"Oh nothing," I said, "but I was just thinking that perhaps you'd like to look at it again. You know we're getting along pretty well now and that sounds like a good
buy. The same house in Halifax would cost at least eight
or nine thousand dollars."

"Hmn," she said, "that's wonderful. There's a letter
for you on the pantry shelf behind the Cream of Wheat
package."

"Sorry, I can't stop to read it now. I have a call to
make. I'll see it when I get back. I just thought you'd be
interested in hearing about the house."

"Perhaps it wouldn't hurt you to read the letter now," she said, looking at me curiously.

Her manner arrested my attention. "All right," I replied, "I'll get it."

It was a long envelope that I picked out from behind the cereal package. One glance at it and my attention came abruptly to focus, for in the upper left-hand corner were printed the words,

———

General Hospital
Neurosurgical Division

I took the letter into the kitchen where Sally was at work, sat down and opened it.

Dear Doctor: [it began]
We have had on file for some time your application for a residency in our neurosurgical service. I wish to inform you that a vacancy is now open.

We have carefully reviewed your qualifications and they appear to be satisfactory. Your experience in general surgery would definitely be of value if you were to come with us.

Doctor C. L. Lee, with whose name you are doubtless familiar, is in need of an assistant at the moment, his former assistant, Doctor Bishop, having had to leave suddenly because of severe ill health.

If you are still interested in coming with us we would be happy to have you. Your decision will have to be made very shortly, however, as we have other applicants, and the position must be filled as soon as possible.

We would appreciate hearing from you by return mail if possible.

> Yours sincerely,
> A. B. SMITH M.D.
> Medical Director,
> ———— General Hospital

To say that I was astonished is to put it mildly. Lee was
one of the foremost brain surgeons on the continent, his
name as familiar to the medical profession as the name
Roosevelt is to the American public. That he, of all men,
should be inviting me to work with him was almost incredible. When I had written the hospital almost two
years before, it had been simply because I had a list of
neurosurgical centers before me and I was covering the
list completely. I had not had the least expectation of a
favorable reply.

I suppose Sally and I read that letter some twenty times
that day, in intervals between my seeing patients in the
office and Sally's feeding the children. I was like a man
in a daze and Sally was nearly as bad. I had been pounding on a door for years and when I least expected it, it
had opened of its own accord.

"Have we the money to do it?" asked Sally at one point.

"It will be tight going," I said, "but I think we could
do it. As a resident the course won't cost me anything.
What we have might be stretched to keep you and the
two children"—long pause—"here."

"Yes, it might," said Sally, in a low and trailing-away
voice, as if she were seeing a ghost.

I could see the ghost too. After waiting and striving so
long, opportunity had come to us, but he had not come
alone. He had brought along a dread companion—the
ghost of separation.

There was only one thing to do, we both agreed, and that was to seize our chance. The letter had said "very shortly." The term was indefinite but I somehow interpreted it to mean about one week. Although our minds were practically made up, I thought I'd wait about that length of time before making the final decision.

During the days that followed I went about my work with a strange feeling of detachment. I saw everything in a new light, as if I were seeing this community for the first time. In James Hilton's book *Lost Horizon* he pictures a sort of earthly paradise lost in the mountains of Tibet. The characters in the story, arriving from the outside world, take a few weeks to realize the nature of the place into which they had been brought. Had I been in this village three years and not realized what it really was? Apart from the physical aspect, Little Brook differed from Shangri-La only in one major respect—the people did not live to be three hundred years old.

Otherwise there was a remarkable similarity. The inhabitants were, almost without exception, prosperous; I think I knew of only two families that could have been called poor. They had no worries about food or housing. They lived on a high level of comfort and security and yet with all this they did not have to work very hard. They had plenty of time for recreation and pleasure. They took everything in moderation, were disturbed about nothing and were as content as human beings can be in this world.

And what was there to explain this happy state of affairs, this prosperity? There were no heavy industries—the shipyard, where they turned out such excellent wooden vessels, was not big. I suppose thirty or forty men were on its normal peacetime payroll. The spruce gum factory with its two or three girls, and the shoe factory employing three or four people besides the family of the man who owned it, could hardly have much effect on the general picture. Nor were there vast tracts of cultivated land yielding marketable and highly profitable crops. Indeed the land looked rather scrubby and the fields were of a size that could easily be worked with one pair of oxen.

No. There was another explanation and I knew what it was, although I had never thought much about it before. It lay in a certain pattern of life. I had viewed this design for living for a long time without appreciating its significance. I had become acquainted with it slowly, over a long period, and its importance had not struck me before.

I reviewed the career, as I knew it, of a typical habitant farmer. Louis, my neighbor, who did so much to help us at the times when we needed help, was a good example.

As a boy Louis had been intelligent, healthy and active. In school he followed the same course of studies as every other schoolboy in Canada. His studies were conducted mostly in French. His teacher was supposed to teach him English, but she was negligent on this score. She knew that he would not need it very much because he was not likely ever to stray far over the boundaries of the community. The boundaries were very well defined. They were not visible from the outside of the community but they were very plainly visible from the inside. They were composed of tradition and a way of life.

When he was not in school, Louis played like any other boy but he also began to learn useful trades. By the time he was sixteen years old he had learned something about carpentry, masonry, lumbering, the care of animals and many other of the hundred and one things he would need to know. When he reached the age of sixteen, his father gave him an acre of land next to his own and also a piece of woodland five or six miles back from the village.

This piece of woodland was the start of Louis' fortune. It was about a quarter of a mile wide and a half mile long. He built a small hut and spent about a month out of every winter cutting logs. He cut only the biggest trees— his father had taught him how to tell when a spruce tree had reached its maximum growth—and he cleared away obstructions which might interfere with the growth of the young saplings. His patch of woodland, in other words, was like a garden to him. He knew that if he took good care of it, it would last him a lifetime. He took from it enough timber each year to give him an income of four or five hundred dollars and no more. By limiting his cut he knew that in old age he would be able to hand it down to one of his sons in as good condition as when he received it.

At the age of seventeen or eighteen he began to think of getting married. With the advice of his father, he decided to build a house. He brought logs to the mill, had them cut into boards—the sawyer taking a percentage of the boards for pay instead of cash—and then hauled them to his acre of land beside his father's house. In his spare time he started the work of building, with the help of his father and his brothers and some of the neighbors. With only part-time labor it took a year or more to build the house, but in the end it was finished and it was a good house. Now he owned his own home completely and outright. For him there would never be any rent to pay.

About the time he began work on his new dwelling he bought a pair of bull calves for twenty dollars. In two years they had grown into a fine pair of oxen. With these he could work his own land and start farming for himself. He could raise almost all the food required for a family, he had a never-ending supply of fuel, an assured income from his wood lot and he owned his own home. He was now in an excellent position to get married, and he did.

As time went on Louis found various ways of increasing his income. He started to raise foxes on a small scale, increased his woodland holdings, and during slack seasons occasionally went "outside" to work as a carpenter. Gradually he built up his income from three figures to four. He knew a good deal about the outside world in spite of the fact that he preferred to stay at home. He learned about investments and such things. He never forgot, however, that his fortunes were rooted in the soil. He taught this to his children when they grew up. When it came time for him to retire he would be able to do for them what his father had done for him.

This then was Louis' life. He had never been obliged to work too hard or to worry too much. He had had plenty of leisure in which to enjoy life in the simple way of his neighbors. He envied no one in the world.

It was a fine existence. Yet for all that, I could not see it as lasting forever, for me; I had too long been nourishing other ideas in my head. I could not so suddenly discard the ambition which I had nurtured for years.

I stood in front of the main entrance to the General Hospital and surveyed an expanse of brick and glass eighteen or nineteen stories high and extending right and left for three or four hundred feet. The lower story as far as I could see, was faced with polished granite—enough for a thousand tombstones—and smooth round pillars four or five feet thick stood on each side of the copper and plate-glass doors. Instinctively I compared it with the two-story, twenty-six bed wooden hospital in Digby in which I had been accustomed to treat my Little Brook patients. It was with some apprehension that I mounted the stone steps.

Just inside the main entrance on the left, in a room as big as an armory, a battalion of girls was at work. Their fingers flew over the keys of typewriters and Comptometers, manipulated recording machines from which they took dictation, sorted papers and filed them here and there in a solid wall of steel filing cabinets. All in all it was a scene of efficiency that would have done credit to General Motors or to a Du Pont factory. I watched them a moment through the open door. They were intelligent pretty girls, working cheerfully—almost gaily, it seemed to me— as they typed and filed away autopsy reports and records of sickness and suffering as if they had been statements of automobiles sold or data pertaining to the manufacture of nylon stockings.

Unquestionably I was in a mood! Somehow the scene gave me a chill. It was, of course, most unreasonable and my better sense told me so, but nevertheless the feeling persisted.

In a small anteroom I found Dr. Smith, the medical superintendent. He was a thin little man, nervous, given to rubber-band smiles, and was the guiding genius behind all the activity in the big room. He was seated at a glass-topped desk on which stood two telephones, a desk blotter and nothing else. He stood up when I came in, welcomed me with a smile and immediately picked up a telephone and told someone in the armory to bring in my file.

I was flattered at their having such a file on me. It was almost an inch in thickness—they had started it two years before when my original letter of application for a residency had been received. It contained a record from every school, college and hospital at which I had studied, letters from medical men of standing in various parts of Nova Scotia, and a summary of my career as kept by the American Medical Association in Chicago. The AMA keeps an accurate biography of every doctor in the United States, the American possessions, and Canada. Let a doctor in Alaska or Newfoundland or in a remote hamlet in the Mississippi Valley take a chew of tobacco and the fact is at once recorded and placed on file in their office. Perhaps this is a slight exaggeration—maybe the doctor would have to chew a whole plug before they would write it down— but the idea at least is true. I don't see how they do it. All in all, I was as thoroughly documented as any resident of Alcatraz, even to fingerprints.

Dr. Smith told me, almost all in one breath, that I was welcome to the hospital, that he would do anything he could to help me, that I would be well advised to have rubber heels put on my shoes to save slipping on the smooth corridors as well as to avoid noise and that Dr. Lee would see me in the coffee room adjacent to Operating Room K 4 at 10.45 A.M. He added that as the hour was now exactly ten-thirty, I had best leave my grips in his office and proceed to this appointment immediately, and he summoned a uniformed porter to escort me. I would be shown to the quarters reserved for me after the interview.

Having stepped off a train not more than an hour before I would have liked to make myself presentable before meeting Dr. Lee but I had no choice. I followed the porter through what seemed like miles of corridors, took an elevator and went up three floors, walked for more miles, turning right and left every little while, and at length came to a door labelled "O.R. K-4 No Admittance." The porter left me and I walked in.

Three men sat in the room. They were dressed in white gowns—slightly bloodied and rumpled, because they had just finished an operation—white shoes, masks pulled down and dangling from their necks, and they were drinking coffee. It was not difficult to pick out Dr. Lee from the group.

Equanimity! The word comes to mind whenever I think of the man who was my chief. To describe him as a man of average height, lean, about fifty years of age with gray eyes and light brown hair, means little. The serene personality of the man was the dominant impression—a personality which shone out so strongly and so steadily that physical details were obscured. The dictionary defines the word "equanimity" as: "[Der. Latin, *aequanimitas. Aequus* equal, + *animus* mind.] Evenness of mind; calmness, firmness or composure of mind, such as is not easily affected or agitated by good or ill fortune." Never have I met anyone so serene and so capable of radiating serenity about him. I was later to see him in every sort of trying situation when I worked with him in the operating room and in the wards, yet I never saw him betray, even by the flicker of an eyelid, any annoyance or irritation.

For some fifteen or twenty minutes Dr. Lee talked with me. He asked me no direct questions about myself—there was no hint of interrogation in the interview—but he talked in general terms about the work, about what it involved, the types of cases which were most commonly dealt with in the neurosurgical service, and finally ended by outlining what my duties were to be.

I came away from this interview with a much better opinion of myself than I had had before. Suddenly I was filled with a certain self-confidence, with a conviction that I could and would master this citadel of science. Already, I told myself, I was well within its ramparts.

My room was one story below ground and was reached by walking such a length of corridors as to make me reflect on the usefulness of bicycles. Rooms opened into it all along the way. From some came the sounds of machinery and the whine of electric motors; from others the chatter of female voices, the owners of which were engaged in occupations strange to me at the moment. Other doors were closed and silent and bore names and notices tacked up on them. I came to my own door and was surprised to see my own name printed on a white card attached to it.

I think I had two simultaneous reactions when I saw this card. To begin with I was flattered, I suppose, at receiving such prompt attention and, unquestionably, it gave me a strong and gratifying sense of belonging, of being part of this great organization. At the same time I was conscious of another feeling which was not so pleasant. The efficiency with which this sign had been printed and put into place within scarcely more than an hour of my arrival, frightened me a little. An organization that was so perfect would demand in turn a high degree of perfection. Precision and orderliness were virtues which I had perhaps failed to cultivate as much as I should have. At that time I even had a certain unreasonable distrust of the methodical notebook type of mind—an attitude no doubt born of my own deficiencies. In Canso I had practiced more than two months before I had got around to having a sign painted. I wished Dr. Smith or whoever was responsible for this card had been a little more lackadaisical. I should have felt more at home.

The room itself was very much like any hotel room. It had a private bath, a desk and a chest of drawers, both with glass tops, and a table lamp beside the bed. But battleship linoleum covered the floor instead of carpeting and the only window, very narrow and near the ceiling, gave light but no view. It was just as well perhaps. When I opened it, I saw nothing but a blank brick wall not more than ten feet away. It was impossible to see the sky.

I do not remember too much of the ordinary day-by-day life at the hospital except for the work I did with Dr. Lee. I met a dozen or more residents who were engaged in other branches of medicine or surgery, scores of junior interns, technicians and nurses. Most of the other residents were younger men than I, had not had any experience in practice on their own and had come directly from medical school to their post-graduate studies. In general they had more "book learning" than I, could quote the medical journals better—they put great store by this and were continually trying to outrival each other in this respect—and knew much more about laboratory techniques. But I thought their views and ideas curiously adolescent in a medical sense. I confess that my experience made me a bit conceited in their presence. In later years many of them were to become leading lights of the profession, far outshining me.

At eight-thirty, the morning after my arrival, I was in Operating Room K 4 ready to assist my chief for the first time.

I suppose the most widely read and popular account of an operation on the brain is in the book called *Hans Brinker or The Silver Skates.* There must be few people in the world, who like books, who have not read this one. Some may regard it as a book for children. Actually it is a more important work than Kant's *Critique of Pure Reason* or Tolstoy's *War and Peace,* just as *Alice in Wonderland* is more important and will live longer than anything ever written by Ernest Hemingway—whom, by the way, I admire intensely. In *The Silver Skates* Hans' father, who has been little more than an idiot for ten years as a result of an accident, is restored to his normal senses in one hour by an operation. The scene is the poorest of poor cottages somewhere in the rural part of Holland.

The great surgeon comes into the sickroom, takes a look at the idiot, talks Latin to his assistant and tells him to open the bag of instruments. With no more preparation they get to work. There is no talk of washing hands, let alone using rubber gloves, no talk of sterile masks or gowns, or, indeed, sterilizing anything. They simply take the instruments out of the bag and get to work. In an hour or so the job is done, in a few minutes more the patient opens his eyes and recognizes his wife and two children for the first time in a decade. He is restored to health. A touching scene follows in the humble cottage, a scene that will draw tears from the most hardened reader. The surgeon takes his leave after ordering a diet of bread, meat and white wine. This may not be realism but it is wonderful just the same.

Our technique was a little different. The first thing we did was to "position" the patient—in my first case it meant turning him so that he lay on his stomach while his face rested on a specially contrived support that allowed him to breathe and yet put no pressure on his nose or chin. This done, his scalp was shaved bare. In the type of surgery to which I had been accustomed, this "prep," as the shaving and cleaning were called, was always done the night before and the patient came to the operating room with the part to be operated upon already well prepared and covered with sterile towels. Dr. Lee explained the reason for this last-minute preparation. Shaving, even when most carefully done, must leave a great many microscopic scratches, if no visible cuts. These scratches were excellent breeding spots for germs, which could multiply very greatly in a matter of twelve hours no matter what antiseptic was applied. After the shaving came the washing with green soap and sterile water, and then the application of a solution of bichloride of mercury. The choice of solution surprised me but when Dr. Lee told me he had got the idea from Dr. Cushing, I thought no more about it; if it was good enough for Cushing it was quite satisfactory to me. This done, a sterile towel was draped over the scalp, and my chief and I went into the scrub room to prepare ourselves.

White pants, white jackets and shoes we had already donned. Now we both put on cotton caps, and two masks, each consisting of four layers of gauze. It is uncomfortable to breathe through eight layers of fine gauze, but it is possible, and not a single germ must escape when breathing over the site of operation. Scrubbing was a fifteen-minute business instead of the customary seven. It left the hands almost raw—I felt as if I had rubbed off an entire layer of skin, like a glove—and made the fingers extraordinarily sensitive when dipped in the strong alcohol bath that followed. When we had on our sterile gowns and sterile rubber gloves we were ready to enter the operating room.

While we had been at this, the anaesthetist had been busily connecting an extraordinary quantity of gadgets to various parts of the patient's anatomy. These devices were joined by wires or by rubber tubes to a number of large-face dials attached to the wall. By watching the dials he could tell at a glance the rate of flow of anaesthetic, the rate and strength of the heartbeat, the body temperature and even the percentage of oxygen entering the patient's lungs along with the rapidity with which it was used. On one side of the operating room and a little above floor level was the gallery, the space from which visiting surgeons could observe what was going on. This area was hermetically sealed off from the operating room by a thick glass partition. No germ-carrying air could pass from it to the place in which we worked. A two-way microphone arrangement made it possible for Dr. Lee to talk to his observers if he so wished, and for them to ask questions on occasion. Altogether it was a rather more elaborate setting than that in which the father of Hans was operated upon.

And now we got to work. The "we" here is, of course, self-flattery, novice that I was. Our patient had a spongioblastoma, one of the most malignant of brain tumors and unfortunately one of the more common, and it was our duty to remove it. Without operation, life expectancy is about three months. With operation we might add a few years to the patient's life, but probably not more than one or two.

When I was a very young doctor I used to wonder about the value of doing surgery in cases where the only benefit was to procure a year or two of more or less vegetable existence for the patient. At first thought a relatively quick death seems preferable to a lingering illness during which life is a burden to the patient and to his relatives. But no good doctor can act on this assumption. The one who does so is a dangerous man. The reason is simple. The best doctor in the world cannot say with absolute certainty that a patient is going to die of a certain illness, no matter what that may be. Because a man has advanced cancer or the most serious type of heart disease, can the most skillful and experienced clinician say with perfect certainty that he is going to die of that condition, and when? No. This may sound like a sweeping statement. So it is, but it is also true. Cancer has been known to disappear of its own accord, to cure itself, so to speak, and people who have been stricken with the most deadly type of heart disease when they were forty or fifty, have lived to be eighty or ninety. There are many mysteries in medicine. Only God can know when and how a person is going to die. A doctor may give an opinion and it may be a very well-founded opinion, but it is no more. He acts on probabilities like the fallible being that he is. No worth-while medical man is ashamed to admit this fact— rather he is grateful that, in the last analysis, a higher Authority takes over.

There are two ways of opening a skull. The choice of method depends largely on the area of brain that must be exposed. When only a small opening is required, a simple drill is used and a hole bored after a flap of scalp has been cut and laid back. The hole can be enlarged to any desired size by the use of a rongeur forceps—a device like scissors with handles that are very thick and strong, and which has, instead of blades, two small spoons of hardened steel with sharp edges which come together when the instrument is manipulated. With this it is easily possible to "gnaw" at the edges of the opening made by the drill, enlarging it as required.

When more room is needed, as in my first case, four holes are drilled at the corners of an imaginary square or parallelogram. This done, a flat flexible strip of platinum is passed through one hole inside the skull, and pushed carefully between the surface of the brain and the inside layer of bone until it appears at another hole where it can easily be seized and drawn through. Attached to this strip of platinum is what looks like a simple steel chain with very fine links, no thicker than a piece of twine. In reality it is a flexible saw and every link is a small sharp tooth, which can be pulled back and forth and the bone sawed through in a matter of seconds. The same is done on all four sides and in a surprisingly short time the square of bone can be lifted off like a cover. It is placed in a basin of isotonic and sterile saline solution and kept covered until the operation is over, when it can easily be replaced.

The tumor did not look very much unlike the surrounding brain tissue. It was soft to the touch, had more little blood vessels on the surface and was fleshy in color. There was a spot near the center that looked like an old blood clot. Dr. Lee put his scalpel into healthy brain tissue just outside the margin of the tumor. Immediately blood appeared.

"Suction," he commanded in a low voice. I applied the end of a pencil-like tube connected by a long rubber hose of small diameter just below the point of incision and the blood was drawn away as rapidly as it flowed.

"Sponge." A small pledget of absorbent cotton of the shape and thickness of a piece of child's crayon was before me. With a forcep I picked it up, touched it to the bleeding area and immediately lifted it again. For a fraction of a second the area was dry. In that brief moment—about one fifth of a second—Dr. Lee grasped the bleeding vessel with a pair of tweezers and held it.

"Endotherm." At the word Miss Wicks touched a copper rod to the tweezers, electric current passed down to the blood vessel and there was a very faint, brief sizzling sound. The end of the vessel had been coagulated and the bleeding stopped.

"Suction, sponge, endotherm," those were the only words spoken—barring a brief and quiet reprimand addressed to me by my chief after the first five minutes—during the next four and a half hours. Doctor Lee was an automaton for the time, Miss Wicks was an automaton and, in a little while, I was an automaton. The reprimand helped me a great deal. "Don't lunge," Dr. Lee said—I was keyed up and anxious to be as alert and quick as possible. "Time your movements to mine and to those of

Miss Wicks. Be neither too quick or too slow. Rhythm is important."

The world disappeared from sight and consciousness. For us the entire universe lay in that two and a half inch square opening, and all the languages on earth were reduced to three or four words. I have tried to describe this absolute concentration before. Four hours passed like four minutes and yet they could as well have been a million years. When we had done and I peeled off my gloves, now wet inside with sweat, and looked around me at ordinary things, saw faces, and smelled coffee it was like awakening into the world for the first time. I drank my cup of coffee, listened to Dr. Lee give me instructions for the afternoon and the next day, and then went off to my room to savor my experience in quiet.

I had sat on a chair, my feet on the bed, for almost an hour, smoking cigarettes and going over in my mind every detail of the operation when an odd thought struck me; with it came some disquieting reflections.

I had just finished my first case, I had helped to remove a spongioblastoma—but who was the patient? His name, address and occupation I knew from the chart of course, but what else did I know about him? What sort of place did he occupy in his community? What were his interests? What kind of wife had he? How did he feel about his children? Did he have any particular worries or problems beyond the immediate one of his illness? How would his living or dying affect his family? In other words, what kind of *person* was he? In his own home he wasn't merely a case! I was shocked at the realization that I had been so absorbed in the tumor that I had forgotten the man.

I suppose I had been at the General Hospital about a month when Anise came into my life.

By that time I had learned a little about neurosurgery and adapted myself pretty well to hospital routine. Dr. Lee threw me an occasional word of praise which I seized upon as hungrily as a dog seizes a bone, relished over and over in the quiet of my room and wrote about in my letters to Sally. Perhaps I exaggerated them a little in writing to her and if she had not had such good sense she might have derived the impression that Dr. Lee was about to let me take over the business of operating on brain tumors entirely. But Sally is a down-to-earth sort of person and I don't think she took my rather glowing accounts too seriously. She sent me replies saying that she was glad I was getting along so well, but also containing the information that Mrs. Zacchary's rheumatism was worse again. Sally had refilled her prescription at least three times; and Josephine à Gustav had brought a baby mink to the house and asked her to prescribe a diet for it. The mink was about two inches long and puny—not at all what a mink of his age should be. Had she done right in prescribing Nestle's milk and Pablum for it? The chief topic in every letter, of course, was the adventures of Ronnie and John. She told me every cute thing they said, described how she had caught Ronnie feeding uncooked bacon rind from the garbage can to John and how they had come to her and seriously asked to know where, if God made all the people in the world, He got all the skin. She had answered the question as best she could only to be confronted five minutes later with the problem of what color was a rat's mouth inside. I thought of Sally and the children a good deal and I know I made a fool of myself several times with the exaggerated attention I paid to little children whom I chanced to meet with their parents in stores and barber shops.

I have no doubt that these letters conditioned me in

part for the impact that Anise was to have on me. But there was another thing, something working in the subconscious every minute of the day and night which was more important still. It was soon to become very clear to me, of course, like other things that we all learn in time through bitter experience. But for that first month, while everything was so new and while I worked with such zeal, there was no room in my mind for anything but the urgency of the moment.

Anise was a patient in Pediatric Ward C-11. She was eight years old and had been brought in from a little village a thousand miles away. I saw her first in company with Dr. Lee when the chief of pediatric department asked him in for a consultation because he thought Anise might be a case for neurosurgery.

C-11 was on the fourteenth floor. It was a fairly large square room with a white ceiling, pink walls covered with drawings of Walt Disney characters plus a few non-Disney elephants and rabbits. There were sixteen small beds in the room, each one with barred sides, and in each was a child somewhere between four and ten years old. A nurse was seated at a desk in the center of the room working on a pile of charts when we came in.

Sixteen pairs of large eyes set in sixteen tiny faces of varying degrees of paleness and thinness, turned on us like a battery of questioning lights. There were children of all descriptions, white, brown and colored, most of them lying down but some sitting or even standing in their cots and holding on to the enameled iron frameworks. Some had bandages on their faces, others had an arm or a leg in plaster cast and one had a rubber tube running into a nostril, which fed her oxygen from a green-painted tank in a rack alongside the bed. Another had an arm strapped down to a board; a container of blood suspended from a frame above her was dripping its contents into a vein. A baby voice from a bed near the door said, "What's your name?" as we entered and another asked Dr. Lee why he didn't have a white coat on.

We found Anise in a corner bed. She was a thin wisp of a thing; the bony prominences of her little frame could be identified without even removing the bedclothes and her features were white and pinched and almost expressionless. Her big brown eyes, looking large as saucers because of the pallor and thinness of her face, alternately shone with a faint gleam of childish interest and became dull with boredom.

After all, she had been in hospital for about a week, been examined by a dozen interns or more in addition to the regular staff doctors, and had submitted to such strange things as blood-sucking needles, enemas, spinal punctures and X-rays. Dr. Lee and I were just two other wearisome strangers come to disturb her. As I looked at her I thought for a moment of my Ronnie and John so far away, scampering about the yard happy and vigorous and screaming excitedly over the capture of a cupful of pollywogs.

My chief said to me, "You speak to her. She knows nothing but French." I put on my best smile, my mildest and most cheerful manner as I addressed her, but I didn't feel like smiling nor did I feel cheerful.

"So you are Anise," I began. "I have a little boy at home just your size. We are new doctors who have come to help you get well. Tell me; how are you feeling?"

She smiled for the first time since we had entered the room. "I am just fine," she told me, "I just have a headache and even that is not too bad. It will go away when I get home. My papa is coming for me soon. Tomorrow I think."

The questioning and examining of Anise took a long

time. Dr. Lee went over her most carefully. After no more than the first minute he had said softly, almost under his breath, "Medulloblastoma, very likely." Nearly an hour passed, during which he read reports on the chart, peered through an opthalmoscope, tested reflexes and went over the nervous system of our patient in detail. It was almost as if he were trying to disprove his own preliminary judgment. At last it was over.

"Medulloblastoma for certain," he said. "Please look after the details of having her transferred to neurosurgical, Doctor. You might stay here and look over these reports carefully yourself. It would be instructive. And I would suggest Boyd again."

Medulloblastoma! A cursed word if ever there was one. Seeing it in print and reading about it in detached fashion a few nights before, it had not seemed so bad—like reading of the explosion on Krakatoa which had happened long ago and so far away. But in connection with the little white face in the corner bed, it was a different matter. The frightfulness in the very ring of the word became apparent. I could easily imagine the devil himself mouthing it with glee. It is one of the most malignant afflictions that can visit a human being—and Anise was talking about going home.

I went over the chart and read the reports from the laboratory and X-ray departments. My little patient was talking as I read, glad to have someone who could understand her language. The writing on the chart became difficult to follow for some reason, as I went on. Words and sentences jumped onto the page and then disappeared of their own accord. There was a yellow slip with which I had special difficulty. It was headed "Report on Spinal Fluid," and it went something like this:

Pressure 260 mm.—I have a little pig with a black spot on his nose and he's all mine my father says I can keep him forever.

Mononuclear leucocytes 22 per cu. mm.—I'd better get home right soon because the other little pigs—we have eight in all—might be mean to him and take all the feed and besides my mother wants me. I know she wants me because I sweep the pantry floor all the time and she needs me to help her dry the dishes and to go over to Tante Louise's when she wants to borrow an onion or something and I can run faster than anybody else in the house even faster than Jules who is in the sixth grade.

Protein 55 mgms. percent—and she needs me to put wood in the firebox I can carry just as big pieces as Jules although not many at a time. Can you do the operation on me now so I will be ready to go home tomorrow with my papa?

I gave up reading and when I said goodbye to Anise I am afraid I was far from professional in my bearing.

The nurse followed me to the door. "I'll phone Miss Carter about the transfer, Doctor," she said. "How do you like our hospital? Have you begun to find your way around yet? Will you be taking in the Saturday evening nurses' dance?"

She was a young and pretty nurse, but I said I didn't think I would be taking in the dance.

Lee operated on Anise the next morning. He had little hope regarding the outcome but he had enough to lead him to undertake the long, fatiguing, delicate operation. It was a beautiful piece of work from a technical viewpoint, but it turned out to be futile. Three days later she went home, but not as she had expected. The little pig with the black spot on its nose did not see her and no doubt had to fend for itself, and if an onion was borrowed or the firebox filled it was done by Jules alone. I suppose there was a pantry to be swept in Heaven.

On the day when the little cot became empty and its mattress was sent down to the mattress-sterilizing room, and the spring and iron framework washed down by two student nurses who chatted gaily to each other all the while about a dance they had attended or were about to attend, and what they wore or intended to wear, a kind of depression came over me. It came to me all of a sudden that this vast hospital, for all the tremendous good it was doing, was as impersonal as a factory. It turned out good deeds on an assembly line basis. Unfairly, of course, I pictured every man and woman in it, every member of the working personnel, as a cog in a great machine; efficient and doing his or her work well, but as indifferent to the end result as a steel cog in a machine that stamps out cakes of soap. I persisted in this unreasonable frame of mind all day and all that evening and I went to bed with a sick feeling, as if a platform on which I had been building for a long time and which had seemed very solid, was about to give way.

The next day I was back to normal again in the sense that I no longer looked at my companions in work as unfeeling machines incapable of human emotion. I knew that they had to acquire a surface impersonality to do their jobs at all.

But something remained—things were not quite as they had been before. Ordinary things appeared in a new light. As I walked down the long corridors, it was as if a voice said to me, "Look how wide and long these corridors are, how smooth the walls, how hard and well polished the floor. Not much like the little crooked hallways of the hospital in Digby! When you get to be a brain surgeon you will walk corridors like these all the time." The long rows of doors on each side were like mouths that said, "Hundreds of people from every part of the world have walked in and out of us. More have walked in than have walked out—but what difference does that make. They are just people." The K-4 sterilizing room with its glitter of chrome fixtures, dials, knobs and handles looked like the control room of a submarine. The four autoclaves themselves with their shining wheels for locking the doors, looked like torpedo tubes, and seemed to say, "How many like us have you in Digby? Not more than one or perhaps two. Hmn. What kind of surgery could you do in a place like that?"

I went for comfort to the neurosurgical wards where I would be among my patients. I looked them over as I came in the door. There was the Retinoblastoma, the Meningioma, the Acoustic Nerve Tumor, the Ependymoma—

It came to me with a queer feeling that I knew all my patients better by the names of their diseases than by their own proper names! It was the common method of designation for patients, even among the nurses. I remember overhearing a student nurse say to one of her companions, "There's the cutest-looking little cerebral palsy in Bed Six. Wait'll you see him." It had struck me as funny at the time, but not now. I had fallen into this common habit myself, unconsciously and by degrees. After all, our patients were all people whom we had never seen before their admission to hospital and would probably never see again after their brief stay. Names like Jones or Smith or Andrews were less distinctive for hospital use than names like Ependymoma and Meningioma.

In our little hospital in Digby, now, the patients had been my neighbors and friends, familiar faces seen on my day-to-day rounds. A man was not merely an appendectomy —he was Pierre whose oxen had pulled my car out of a ditch when I was stuck, who brought hardwood to my house, and whose wife I had delivered of twins. Jules à Desirée whose gall bladder I was about to remove was the neighbor who sold us eggs and who came to the house to help when Ronnie was sick.

But this would be no more. A specialist in brain surgery must live in a large city, and work in a hospital like this one. His patients must come from many distant points and, except in the very unusual case, be perfect strangers to him. His relationship to them must be always scientific. He has no time to become a friend to his patients. He cannot deliver a brand-new baby, give antitoxin to a child with diphtheria, and certainly no one will ask him to operate on an ox with a torn shoulder or on a dog whose leg has been run over by a cart.

I began to wonder whether I was, after all, suited to the life of a city specialist.

Weeks went by, during which I argued with myself that an ambition of so many years standing should not be given up lightly. I worked harder than ever, saw my patients a dozen times a day, studied neurology until my eyes burned in my head, and did my best to get myself into the detached frame of mind, the impersonal attitude towards patients which I must have in order to be a good brain surgeon. But I did not succeed. In the end it was my chief himself who, unknowingly, put an end to the mental struggle.

We were drinking coffee in the dressing room one day when he paid me one of his rare compliments.

"You're not doing too badly, Doctor," he said. "I think

in a month or so you'll be ready to do a few things on your own. You should be able to handle something like, let us say, sectioning the sensory root of the gasserian ganglion."

A month before those words would have been more than enough to raise me up to the seventh pinnacle. They would have had the effect which my chief intended—a terrific boost to my morale and fuel to the fires of my ambition. But now, although I was pleased at the compliment, they had an opposite effect. I think it was at this moment that the dream finally dissolved—as dreams have a way of doing when we taste the actuality.

That night, alone in my room, I admitted to myself for the first time that I did not want to be a brain surgeon.

Babies with croup, old people worried about their hearts and their blood pressure, young people with day-to-day maladies and injuries—these were my responsibilities. Little Brook was my sphere—not the city.

Next morning, after a frontal lobe division, my chief listened to my story with his customary calm. When I had finished he asked me a few questions, and I will always be grateful that he attempted to change my way of thinking, that he wanted me to remain.

I remember very well what he said at the last.

"Stay a few weeks more, Doctor, until we have Doctor Reals well started in your place, and while you think it over a little more. In that way you won't blame yourself later for making the decision too suddenly." And then he added, "Actually, I must confess, I almost envy you. . . ."

A month later, on the outbound train the thought came to me, that trains are really very wonderful things, just as if I had never been on one before. But this one was taking me home.

Someday, I knew, we would leave our Acadian Shangri-La, and the people there—the Moises, Hilarion, his father-in-law, Peter and Matilda Barnett, Pierre, Louis, the women I had attended in childbirth and the children—they would have another doctor to call out in the middle of cold winter nights or just as he had settled down to a longed-for evening at home. But it would not be because I had attained a great and—I still think with satisfaction—honorable ambition. It would be because I had simply gone from one place to another place, knowing that wherever I may be I shall find people to take care of, and to care about.

But in the meantime, the train was carrying me back where I belonged, with Sally and the children, and I hoped there would always be one of those wonderful contraptions to do the same thing for me if we were ever separated again. And I hoped Sally would remember to have some bottles of cider in the house—I was not much worried that she would forget—for this was the kind of homecoming that called for a celebration.